Standard of Care

A REAL ESTATE AGENT'S GUIDE TO RISK MANAGEMENT

James B. McKenney
Attorney at Law

Professional Publishing
122 Paul Drive, San Rafael, CA 94903

Please Note: This book is designed to provide accurate and authoritative information in regard to the subject covered. However, such information may not be sufficient in dealing with a client's particular real estate situation, and the author does not warrant or represent its suitability for such purpose. Persons using this material do so with the understanding that the author does not intend to render legal, accounting, real estate or other professional services; and that the information provided herein should not be relied upon as a substitute for independent research and consultation with lawyers, accountants and real estate licensees. If legal advice or other expert assistance is required, the services of a competent professional person should be sought. The publisher and author assume no responsibility for errors or omissions or assume any liability for damages resulting from the use of the information contained herein.

CAUTION: IT IS NOT THE INTENT OF THE AUTHOR TO ESTABLISH A LICENSEE'S STANDARD OF CARE FOR A PARTICULAR SITUATION. RATHER, IT IS THE AUTHOR'S INTENT TO ADVISE LICENSEES TO ACT IN A MANNER WHICH MAY BE WELL ABOVE THE STANDARD OF CARE IN ORDER TO AVOID CLAIMS HAVING MERIT AS WELL AS THOSE WITHOUT MERIT.

International Standard Book Number 1-885104-00-6

Manuscript Editors

Paul Chaffee, James Little,
George and Susan Gazulis,
Judith McKenney

Cite Checking

Wendy Behrens, Kathy Kugelmas

Cover Designer

Roz Stendahl, Dapper Design

PROFESSIONAL PUBLISHING

122 Paul Drive, San Rafael, CA 94903 (800) 288-2006

$\mathscr{C}$ONTENTS

Part I

The Threat of Litigation

A. Risk Management

On rare occasions a lawsuit arises out of a real estate transaction no matter how careful or prudent the participants may be. Most often, however, the controversy occurs because one of the principals is either careless or intentionally deceives the other. The agent who fails to discover the error, misrepresentation or concealment is often found to have deviated from the ordinary Standard of Care and shares liability along with the principal.

"Risk management" is the conscious effort to engage in conduct which minimizes such exposure and, if ensnared in litigation, to make certain that the financial responsibility for handling that litigation and settling the dispute rests with the supervising broker. To the broker, risk management means the careful training, supervision and control of agents to keep exposure within reasonable and budgeted boundaries. Even with the comforting umbrella of adequate errors and omissions insurance coverage, it is important that the brokerage establish and maintain a reputation for its technical as well as marketing skills. Risk management also entails retaining competent and imaginative legal counsel to make certain the company and agents are properly advised and protected at all stages of any controversy.

Experience teaches us that most litigation involves strikingly similar factual situations. Of all lawsuits filed, ninety percent fall into areas that can be predicted and avoided. Often the press of time, the emotional desire to nail down the deal, failure to communicate, lack of experience, or simple carelessness exposes the agent and the agent's broker to liability. The object of this manual is to identify these areas and assist the agent in developing a course of conduct within the "Standard of Care." Failure to act within the Standard of Care not only leads to the refund of any commission earned but can result in substantial additional damages.

1

Frequently, the agent and broker are sued for intentional fraud as well as professional negligence or negligent misrepresentation. On occasion, a jury finds the agent guilty of fraud, with serious consequences that cannot be relieved by errors and omissions insurance. During a trial the "truth" is determined only by the evidence that the jury is *allowed* to consider. Testimony of the star witness against the real estate agent is often received without any knowledge on the part of the jury that the witness is a habitual liar. Jurors often cannot comprehend complicated instructions defining the necessary elements of "fraud" and "deceit," which are given to them in the monotonous voice of a judge who has tired of the whole case.[1] Since many jurors harbor the belief that real estate agents earn huge commissions for doing nothing, they may well find fraud in order to punish an agent who was really only negligent. Consequently, it is important to consider conduct which can minimize the exposure of a finding of intentional misrepresentation or concealment, even though dishonesty is the furthest thing from an agent's mind.

2

B. The Probability of Getting Sued

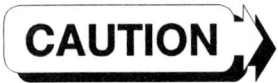

CAUTION

Whether you are new to the real estate industry or an old hand and in the process of changing brokers, the first question to ask your prospective broker is not what it is offering by way of a commission split. Instead ask about the broker's provision for errors and omissions coverage! Many licensees find out too late that they took coverage for granted when it was not there or — and this happens much too frequently — they did not understand the various limitations on this necessary protection.

In the thirty years the author has been defending real estate brokers and agents, there have been dramatic shifts in the level of exposure to litigation. In the 1960s purchase agreements were simple, often consisting of no more than one page. Agents were considered "middlemen," who found buyers for property they listed. The negotiations were up to the principals and agents were mere scriveners. Indeed, the bar association protested loudly whenever they thought real estate agents were getting too involved in drafting purchase agreements. Most properties were

---

[1]Fortunately, jurors may now request that they also receive instructions in written form. Some judges permit a copy to be sent in for each juror. Others only permit one copy to be brought into the jury room.

sold "as is," and sellers seemed under no particular duty to reveal defects that they might be aware of. The phrase *caveat emptor* — "let the buyer beware" — was the canon of the day.

1. The Easton Doctrine

The 1970s ushered in the concept of consumer protection and, toward the end of the decade, suits for fraud and misrepresentation in the sale of real property — particularly residential property — began to proliferate. Often the buyer's agent was included in the action for professional negligence in not advising the purchaser of possible pitfalls in the purchase. On February 22, 1984, the California Court of Appeal in the *Easton v. Strassburger*[2] case surprisingly announced that even the **agent of the seller has a duty to inspect the property and warn the purchaser of possible defects.** The decision, in effect, created a new duty running from the seller's agent to the buyer. In addition, for the first time an agent was held liable for failing to disclose information that he or she was not aware of but would have been aware of if the agent had made a reasonably competent inspection of the premises.

The *Easton* case brought the issue of disclosure to the forefront of the real estate industry. A new civil wrong had been created, and it did not take long for lawyers to catch on and strengthen their financial bottom line. For a period of time the flow of litigation increased, though not in a frenzied pace. Many of us felt the rapid appreciation in value of the property embarrassed most buyers from pursuing damages for imagined or real defects in the property.

While the market was flat, most aggrieved buyers chose to rescind the contract, that is, to put the parties back in the same position as existed before the sale took place. This included the agents who ordinarily must return their commissions if the rescission action is successful. When real estate began to appreciate, buyers chose the alternate remedy of damages for the torts of intentional misrepresentation, concealment, or negligent misrepresentation. Agents were customarily charged with professional negligence and breach of fiduciary duty in addition to the fraud causes of action. Courts held that the

3

---

[2](1984) 152 Cal.App.3d 90; 199 Cal.Rptr. 383.

concept of "let the buyer beware" was an anachronism in California, having little or no application in real estate law.[3]

As soon as the market started to flatten out, buyers took less comfort in the substantial appreciation they had previously enjoyed, and lawsuits were filed at a rapidly increasing rate. Brokers, who had previously experienced two or three lawsuits a year, were finding themselves defending two or three suits every month. The legislature, concluding that *Easton* was "imprecise and confusing,"[4] moved to stabilize the situation with passage of Civil Code sections 2079 to 2079.5, spelling out precisely what this new duty was and the Standard of Care to be applied.

A year later, the legislature introduced the **Transfer Disclosure Statement**.[5] This disclosure statement, often referred to as the "TDS," has become the most significant document in the sales transaction, drawing more attention and creating more controversy than the agreement of sale itself. One of its most laudatory effects was an immediate and significant reduction in litigation.

Some skeptics insist that you do not have lawsuits when the market is down. History does not support this theory. If anything, a weak market seems to stimulate litigation. There seems to be no reasonable explanation for the current decrease in litigation other than the introduction of the Transfer Disclosure Statement. Indeed, most of the lawsuits now filed result from claims on the part of buyers that the sellers and the sellers' agents have either negligently or intentionally made errors in the TDS. Buyers' agents are frequently brought in on the theory that they should have verified the representations in the Transfer Disclosure Statement that the buyers claim are false.

Even if the litigation explosion is brought under control, the probability of a productive agent being sued is still relatively high. In an informal poll taken among counsel for leading residential real estate brokers, it appears that one to two percent of all closings will wind up in litigation. While this might appear minuscule at first glance, a large brokerage firm can easily close 2000 transactions per year. This means 20 lawsuits a year, which adds up to a substantial exposure. It has also been

4

[3]*Alexander v. McKnight* (1992) 7 Cal.App.4th 973; 9 Cal.Rptr.2d 453.

[4]Stats. 1985, Ch. 223, §4, p. 541.

[5]Civil Code §§1102 *et seq.*

estimated, albeit unscientifically, that within ten years the chance of a good producer being named as a defendant in litigation is about 90 percent. No one is immune from the threat of litigation. It is as important as ever to avoid the traps leading to an agent being named a litigant.

While *Easton* and the required disclosure form have been confined to residential sales,[6] the same concept of disclosure is finding its way into commercial transactions. For example, one court has held that the owner of commercial property owes a duty of disclosure to a lessee regarding matters affecting the desirability of the premises.[7] **It is recommended, although not required, that the Transfer Disclosure Statement also be used in commercial transactions.**

RECOMMEND

2. Statute of Limitations

In order to limit the length of time a person is exposed to litigation for his or her wrongful conduct, various statutes of limitation have been enacted. They prescribe a time within which an action must be commenced after it "accrues" or is forever barred. Generally, a cause of action "accrues" when the wrongful act is done and liability arises.[8] However, this rule is ameliorated when it would be unjust to deprive a plaintiff of a cause of action before he or she is **aware** of the injury. Consequently, most statutes of limitation are governed by the discovery rule. That is, the time period does not commence until the plaintiff has notice or information which would put a reasonable person on notice. This is called the "**delayed discovery rule**."

Statutes of limitations that licensees should be aware of are:

▶ **10 years** — Code of Civil Procedure section 337.15 provides a ten-year limitation period for suits for latent defects in improvements to real property. The statute runs from the date of substantial completion, and the delayed discovery rule does not apply. It has been held that this statute also bars claims for indemnity unless brought within the 10-year

5

---

[6]Civil Code §§1102 *et seq.* apply only to a transaction involving one to four residential units.

[7]*Moradzadeh v. Antonio* (1992) 7 Cal.Rptr.2d 475. However, the opinion has been depublished and cannot be cited as authority.

[8]*Menefee v. Ostawari* (1991) 228 Cal.App. 3d 239; 278 Cal.Rptr. 805.

period.[9] The idea is to terminate what was endless exposure for developers, architects and others involved in subdivisions and like projects. Prior to the enactment of this statute, the delayed discovery rule allowed lawsuits to be brought for construction defects decades after a project had been completed.

▶ **4 years** — Actions for breach of a written contract must be brought within four years from the date of the breach. This would normally involve an alleged breach by the agent of the listing agreement. For example, the seller might claim that the agent failed to make any reasonable effort to sell the property. Actions are rarely brought on this theory.

▶ **3 years** — Causes of action for fraud and deceit, including intentional misrepresentation, intentional concealment, and negligent misrepresentation must be brought within three years after date of discovery.[10]

▶ **3 years** — Causes of action of breach of fiduciary duty must be brought within three years of date of discovery.[11]

▶ **3 years** — The Department of Real Estate also has limitations in seeking to impose disciplinary proceedings. Business & Professions Code section 10101 provides that an accusation must be filed within three years of the act giving rise to the disciplinary proceeding or, in the case of charges of fraud or misrepresentation, within one year after discovery or three years from the act, whichever is later, but in no event later than ten years. Where an agent or broker is found liable for fraud in a civil action, the 3-year period runs from the date the judgment becomes final and not from the date of the act giving rise to the litigation.[12]

▶ **2 years** — Actions for professional negligence are governed by a two-year statute which runs from date of discovery.[13] If the alleged negligence is a violation of the duty to make a

6

---

[9]*Time for Living, Inc. v. Guy Hatfield Homes/All American Development Co.* (1991) 230 Cal.App.3d 30; 280 Cal.Rptr. 904.

[10]Calif. Code of Civil Procedure §338(d).

[11]*Stalberg v. Western Title Ins. Co.* (1991) 230 Cal.App.2d 1223; 282 Cal.Rptr. 43.

[12]*California Real Estate Loans, Inc. v. Wallace* (1993) 18 Cal.App.4th 1575; 23 Cal.Rptr.2d 462.

[13]3 Witkin, California Procedure (3d ed. 1985) Actions, §440, p. 470.

visual inspection of the premises, the two years runs from the date of recordation, date of possession, or close of escrow, whichever occurs first.[14]

▶ **1 year** — Any claims for personal injury, including emotional distress, arising out of a defective condition of the property must be brought within one year.[15]

C. Why Insurance?

There is something unsettling about being served with a summons and complaint while you are having a peaceful dinner. Even worse is explaining to your loved ones why you are accused of being a cheat, swindler, liar and generally despicable person causing tens of thousands of dollars of damage to an unsuspecting and innocent party in a real estate transaction! That your manager is backing you all the way, and the lawyer retained to defend you is sympathetic, helps but cannot relieve all the anxiety. You spend time reviewing the transaction; trying to remember what happened and when; regretting that you did not keep better notes of what was said; being prepped for your deposition; and then answering questions from a hostile and intimidating attorney under oath. While all of this is unfortunate, it is nothing compared with the tragedy that could happen if you had to pay the bill. And it is not the amount in controversy that is so critical — however devastating. It is the attorney's fees. Of the budget large brokerage firms set up for litigation, ten percent is allocated for the payment of claims, and an astonishing ninety percent for the cost of defending them. While this is not to denigrate attorneys generally, the reality is that run-amok lawyers are a far greater threat to your well being than the claims of disgruntled buyers or sellers.

A typical example can be found in a Marin County case. The California Supreme Court recently denied a petition for review, ending all further appeals in the seven-year old complaint.

John and Georgiana Schreck, a pleasant, unassuming couple each 70 years old, owned an undeveloped lot in San Anselmo,

7

---

[14]Calif. Civil Code §2079.4.

[15]*Miller v. Lakeside Village Condominium Assn.* (1991) 1 Cal.App.4th 1611, 2 Cal.Rptr.2d 796.

Marin County. They retired to Chico and hoped to sell the lot and use the proceeds as part of their retirement fund. In 1986 they listed the lot with a well-known local broker. They did not often visit the lot and were unaware that the next door neighbors had used an old concrete pad on the lot from time to time to barbecue and as a play area for their child. The neighbors had purchased their house three years earlier.

The Schrecks got an offer from a minister who wanted to build a house on the lot for himself and his family. The Schrecks previously had soil tests conducted and plans prepared for a house which had been approved by the Town of San Anselmo. The Schrecks and the prospective purchasers both were confident that a building permit could be obtained without difficulty. The agreed upon purchase price was $49,500, of which the Schrecks were to pay a 10 percent commission for sale of raw land.

Shortly before the scheduled close of escrow, the minister was standing on the property with his wife discussing the plans for their new house. The neighbor opened the window and shouted "What are you doing there — that is my property." A discussion ensued and, by making some crude measurements, it became apparent that the property was not included within the neighbor's lot. Nevertheless, the Schrecks paid for a formal survey which indeed did show that the old concrete pad was in the middle of their lot and the neighbors had in fact been trespassing.

The neighbors refused to concede, however, and told the minister they would do everything possible to bar his developing the land since they felt it must be theirs. The attorney for the minister advised him not to go through with the deal because he was just "buying a lawsuit." Schreck then filed a quiet title action against the neighbor and also sued for trespass and interference with his contractual relationship with the minister.

The neighbors counter-sued, claiming that they had acquired a prescriptive easement, despite the fact that they had not even occupied the property for the requisite five years.[16] They filed a separate action against the previous owner of their house, that

8

---

[16]To acquire a prescriptive easement the claimant must prove open and notorious use; continuous and uninterrupted use; use hostile to the true owner; and use for the statutory period of five years. Calif. Civil Code § 1007; Calif. Code of Civil Procedure § 321; *Otay Water Dist. v. Beckwith* (1991) 1 Cal.App.4th 1041; 3 Cal.Rptr.2d 223.

seller's broker, and their own broker, claiming they had each been guilty of misrepresenting the property line.

At this stage of the controversy, the matter could easily have been settled if the neighbors, or the brokers on their behalf, had purchased the lot from the Schrecks for the original contract price of $49,500. By the time the trial was concluded, the Schrecks had spent $60,000 in attorney's fees; the seller $30,000 (they settled during the course of the trial); the listing agent $73,000; the selling agent $54,000; and the neighbors $109,000. The total fees at the conclusion of the trial came to $326,000. The jury granted the Schrecks quiet title to their property and damages in the sum of $104,000. They did not award damages against either of the agents involved in the sale to the neighbors.

The Court of Appeal confirmed the jury verdict, and a petition for review was denied by the Supreme Court, but not until the parties had spent another $90,000 for the preparation of the record and appeal and the appellate briefs. Consequently, over $400,000 was spent trying to resolve a $49,500 claim. Mrs. Schreck died shortly before the case became final. This type of horror story can be repeated time and time again. Indeed, of the 20 or more jury cases that the author has tried in the last several years, the attorney's fees have always exceeded the amount in controversy by several times.

CAUTION

In tort cases (those involving negligence or fraud) as opposed to breach of contact cases, each party is usually responsible for his or her own attorney fees. Some real estate contracts, however, contain printed provisions which provide that in the event of any dispute "arising out of the sale," the prevailing party, including the agents, are entitled to reasonable attorney fees. Language such as this has been held broad enough to permit recovery of attorney fees by and against the buyer and seller even on tort causes of action.[17] One case even suggests that such broad language permits recovery of attorney fees against the agent.[18] While this is great if you win, the exposure if you lose is enormous. Make certain the attorney fee clause in the buy-sell agreement does not refer to the agent or broker in any way.

9

---

[17]*3250 Wilshire Blvd. Bldg. v. W.R. Grace & Co.* (9th Cir. 1993) 990 F.2d 487; *Lerner v. Ward* (1993) 13 Cal.App.4th 155; 16 Cal.Rptr.2d 486.

[18]*Xuereb v. Marcus & Millichap, Inc.* (1992) 3 Cal.App.4th 1338; 5 Cal.Rptr.2d 154. But the result may have been impliedly overruled in *Super 7 Motel Associates v. Wang* (1993) 16 Cal.App.4th 541; 20 Cal.Rptr.2d 193.

The burden of defending litigation is impossible for the ordinary real estate agent to meet without insurance of some kind. Without coverage, bankruptcy is often the only solution — and this does not discharge judgments based on fraud.

D. Types of Coverage

10

Frequently, the broker has available for its agents errors and omissions insurance with a known insurance carrier. Policies normally fall into three categories:

▸ First, all policies provide that the act constituting the error or omission must occur during the policy period. The courts hold that "occurrence" is not necessarily when the wrongful act was committed, but rather when the complaining party was actually damaged.

▸ Second, some policies provide that there must be an occurrence and a "claims made" during the policy period. This has been defined to mean that a demand for money or services has been made against and received by the insured.

▸ Finally, a few policies require an occurrence, a claim made, and a "claim reported" to the insurance carrier during the policy period. This means the insured must put the insurance company on notice of the claim before the policy is terminated or lapses. If a policy is about to terminate, brokers will frequently ask their agents to prepare a list of any possible claims pending and report these to the carrier.

A policy will not cover occurrences prior to the beginning of the policy period unless it specifically provides that "prior acts" are covered. If they are, the policy usually inserts a date prior to the beginning of the policy and an extra premium is charged. Similarly, if a policy is to be terminated, the insured has the option of purchasing a "tail coverage," permitting claims to be reported after the policy period provided that the act giving rise to the claim occurred during the policy period.

The type of policy the broker has becomes most important when the agent shifts his or her license to another broker. What happens, for instance, if the first broker goes broke and his E & O policy is terminated? If it is a "claims made" type of policy, one which requires the claim to be submitted during the policy period, the agent is out of luck. In one case the broker went out of business and a claim was then filed against the broker and

CAUTION ▸

two of its agents who were the listing and selling agents on a residential property sale. The seller had taken back a purchase money deed of trust which, she claimed, the agents had permitted her to subordinate to a new first deed of trust which the buyer had obtained during the course of the escrow. The total mortgages were greater than the value of the property. The buyer, after taking a substantial chunk of the refinanced first deed of trust, did not make any payments on either the first or the seller carry-back second. The seller was wiped out and sued the agents on the ground that they negligently permitted her to enter into the transaction. The Independent Associate Agreement signed by the agents with the broker gave the agents full indemnity. However, when the broker went bust — the protection evaporated. Since the liability of the agents was obvious, they were forced to place second mortgages on their homes to get sufficient cash for a settlement. Today, five years later, they are still paying off those second mortgages.

Before you become associated with a broker, ask these questions. This is no time to be shy! If you are not satisfied with the answers, hang your license with someone else.

RECOMMEND

✓ Does the broker have errors and omissions insurance? Is it a real policy underwritten by an insurance carrier or is it a self-insurance type coverage?

✓ If the broker is self-insured, are the contributions made by the agents kept in a segregated fund or are they commingled? If commingled, you have no assurance that the fund will remain solvent.

✓ If there is an insurance carrier, what is the deductible? Some policies have a deductible of $100,000 or more. This is not really E & O coverage, but catastrophic coverage. How does the broker intend to cover the deductible? A deductible of $5,000 to $15,000 is considered safe.

✓ Review the policy exclusions. Will your specialty be insured? Common exclusions include property management, mortgage brokerage, and commercial-investment brokerage.

✓ If you terminate with the broker, are you covered for claims made after you leave arising out of prior transactions? This is sometimes called a "tail coverage." Some brokers charge a modest fee for this coverage when you terminate. The indemnity provided is well worth the cost.

11

✓ Who selects the attorney that will defend you — the insurance carrier or the broker? Except in the case of a conflict of interest, the agent rarely has the opportunity to select the attorney. An attorney selected by the broker is usually preferable because he will be involved for the long term and will be much more available and supportive.[19]

✓ If there is a claim for punitive damages or some other claim which might give rise to a conflict between you and the broker, can you select your own attorney? If so, who pays the fees?

✓ Does the broker provide regular legal updates from the company counsel to apprise you of changes in the law affecting risk management and the Standard of Care?

While there are no "right" answers to all of these questions, it is important to know exactly where you stand when that complaint is served upon you.

12

E. The Independent Associate Agreement

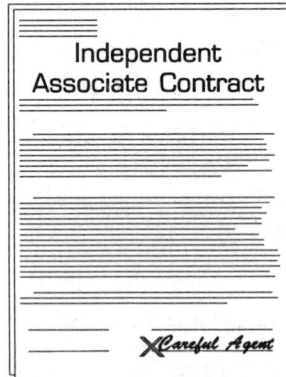

The regulations of the Department of Real Estate require that each licensee have a written employment agreement with the broker setting forth the material aspects of the relationship between the parties, including supervision of licensed activities, duties and compensation.[20] The agreement must be kept available for inspection for three years following termination of the relationship. It is recommended, however, that a fully executed copy of the agreement be kept in

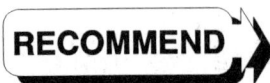

RECOMMEND

---

[19]But see the discussion of *Cumis* counsel, page 14, *infra.*

[20]Title 10 California Code of Regulations, §2726.

your permanent files. It may be helpful in situations arising many years after the employment has been terminated.

In past years, it was considered important for tax and other reasons that the agent be classified as an "independent contractor." Consequently, broker-agent employment agreements are often labeled "Independent Associate Agreements" or use similar terminology. However, the contents of the agreement rather than its label determines the relationship between the parties.[21]

Oddly enough, a salesperson may be an employee for some purposes and an independent contractor for others. For example, a real estate salesperson is no longer considered an employee for federal income tax purposes if paid by commission rather than an hourly rate and if the contract with the broker specifies that the agent is not an employee for tax purposes.[22] This eliminates the need for withholding income and social security taxes. Nor is the salesperson an employee for purposes of unemployment insurance[23] or the application of minimum wage laws.[24]

For purposes of the application of California real estate law and regulations, the agent is considered an employee of the broker.[25] This is because the broker is required by law to supervise the activities of the salesperson, one of the critical indications of an employer-employee relationship. However, court cases have been divided as to whether an agent is an employee for the purposes of coverage under the Workers' Compensation Law. One case held that the supervision required by the regulations and statutes is not, in itself, sufficent to create the relationship of employer and employee. However, the case was ordered depublished by the California Supreme Court and cannot be cited as authority.[26] To avoid the hassle and the uncertainty, most prudent brokers purchase workers' compensation insurance to cover their salespersons.

13

---

[21] *Toyota Motor Sales U.S.A., Inc. v. Superior Court* (1990) 220 Cal.App.3d 864, 877; 269 Cal.Rptr. 647, 654.

[22] Internal Revenue Code §3508.

[23] California Unemployment Insurance Code §650.

[24] *Grubb & Ellis Co. v. Spengler* (1983) 143 Cal.App.3d 890, 895; 192 Cal.Rptr. 637, 640.

[25] See *Grubb & Ellis Co. v. Spengler, supra* footnote 24.

[26] *Aschwanden v. Workers' Comp. Appeals Bd.* (1991) 281 Cal.Rptr. 182; ordered depublished August 1991.

The fact that salespersons are usually considered agents and not employees works to their disadvantage in the event that the broker goes into bankruptcy. Employees have a preference putting them at the head of the line in sharing whatever assets are available. Currently, independent sales agents do not share in the bankruptcy estate in the same manner that employees do. A currently pending amendment to the Bankruptcy Code §507 would give priority to claims of independent sales agents as well.

While the difference between "employee" and "independent contractor" can be compared *ad infinitum,* the difference has little or no significance in litigation involving the Standard of Care.

1. Tendering a Defense

14

CAUTION

In addition to provisions covering the term, compensation and duties of the parties, the Independent Associate Agreement should set forth in detail the rights and obligations of the parties in the event of third-party claims, that is, an errors and omissions section. At a minimum, the following items should be covered:

First, the broker should agree to pay all cost and expense incurred in providing the salesperson with a defense. This includes lawyers' fees, filing fees, deposition costs, and similar expenses. Normally, the broker has the right to select the lawyer, and often special compensation arrangements are made with a firm that handles all of the broker's litigation. The agent is entitled to a competent defense, and usually the lawyer selected by the broker has extensive experience and expertise in the field. With true errors and omissions insurance coverage, the insurance carrier may have the right to select the attorney.

If a conflict arises whereby the attorney selected by the broker or the insurance carrier cannot adequately represent the agent, the agent is entitled to *"Cumis"* counsel, named after the case first recognizing this right.[27] In that case the insurer provided counsel but sent a "reservation of rights" letter denying any liability for punitive damages and reserving its responsibility to pay a judgment on certain causes of action which it felt were not covered by the policy. The court held that this created a conflict of interest on the part of the attorney and that the

---

[27] *San Diego Navy Federal Credit Union v. Cumis Ins. Society, Inc.* (1984) 162 Cal.App.3d 358; 208 Cal.Rptr. 494.

insurance company was obligated to pay for an independent counsel hired by the insured, who was entitled to take charge of the defense.

This right has now been codified in Civil Code section 2860 which provides that where a conflict of interest arises, the insurer shall provide independent counsel to represent the insured unless this right is expressly waived in writing. Under the statute a conflict arises when the insurer reserves rights on a given issue. An allegation of punitive damages does not, in itself, create a conflict according to the statute. In real estate litigation, however, it is hard to imagine how a conflict can be avoided where the plaintiff seeks punitive damages. The broker, in order to escape liability, will always claim it was ignorant of and never ratified the agent's conduct, leaving the agent to "twist in the wind." Surely, this constitutes a conflict.

Some Independent Associate Agreements provide that if the agent desires *Cumis* counsel, the agent is responsible for compensating that counsel. The validity of such provisions in the context of real estate broker-agent contracts has not yet been tested in the courts. It would seem that if a carrier is providing the attorney, then whether the agent must pay for *Cumis* counsel would depend strictly on whether the provisions of the above-quoted statute apply. If a carrier is not involved, the question is open.

15

The application of Labor Code section 2802 is also a possibility that has not been fully addressed by the courts in the context of real estate litigation. This section provides:

> An employer shall indemnify his employee for all that the employee necessarily expends or loses in direct consequence of the discharge of his duties as such, or of his obedience to the directions of the employer, even though unlawful, unless the employee, at the time of obeying such directions, believed them to be unlawful.

Since the agent is considered an employee of the broker for real estate purposes, one might expect the Labor Code to require the broker to provide the agent with counsel in all lawsuits. In a case not related to real estate brokers, one court held that if there is a conflict of interest between the employer and the employee, or if counsel is not provided in a timely fashion, or is incompetent, the employee is entitled to be reimbursed for attorney fees that he "necessarily expends" in hiring his own lawyer.[28] The court was careful, however, to note it was not extending the "Cumis" doctrine, but was merely applying the provisions of the Labor Code. Whether this Labor Code provision will be applied to give real estate licensees additional protection from financial loss (perhaps even in fraud cases), will have to await a decision on point.

2. Indemnifying the Agent

16

Clearly, the Independent Associate Agreement should contain a provision holding the agent harmless from any judgment that might be rendered against the agent for professional negligence, negligent misrepresentation, breach of fiduciary duty or, in those rare cases when it is pled, for breach of contract. However, there is considerable dispute about indemnifying the agent against judgments for fraud, that is, intentional misrepresentation or concealment. (While negligent misrepresentation in California is sometimes classified as fraud and deceit, for purposes of indemnification there seems to be agreement the agent is entitled to be protected.)

The Insurance Code in California specifically prohibits coverage for intentional acts of fraud.[29] Relying upon this provision, many brokers say they will not tender a defense or indemnify an agent who is accused of intentional fraud. But the agent is never sued just for fraud. There are always several causes of action, usually including one for professional negligence and/or negligent misrepresentation. How can a lawyer defend only half a case? Similarly, unless special interrogatories are submitted to the jury specifically asking them to determine whether the defendants were guilty of fraud, negligence or both, you cannot tell from a general verdict the basis on which the jury awarded damages.

It seems clear that where the claim or complaint combines allegations of both negligence and intentional tort, the broker has a duty to provide the agent with a defense for all of the causes of action. When it comes to paying the judgment, however, the broker can justifiably refuse to pay that portion of

---

[28]*Grissom v. Vons Companies, Inc.* (1991) 1 Cal.App.4th 52; 1 Cal.Rptr.2d 808.

[29]Calif. Insurance Code §533 provides: "An insurer is not liable for a loss caused by the wilful act of the insured. . . ."

the judgment identified as resulting from intentional fraud. This is particularly true when punitive damages have been awarded by the jury.

Punitive damages, or damages intended to punish a defendant, are allowed where the plaintiff proves by clear and convincing evidence (as opposed to the preponderance of the evidence ordinarily required) the defendant was guilty of fraud, oppression, or malice. These damages are based, in large part, on the net worth and income of the offending party and must be specifically stated by the jury. The broker has no duty to pay these damages.

Whether the broker is liable to pay the plaintiff's attorneys fees in fraud cases has never been tested in the courts. Attorney fees are now usually treated as "costs" rather than "damages," and are fixed by the court after trial. An argument can be made that since the attorney fees are awarded separately from the fraud judgment, the broker is responsible to indemnify the agent from any attorney fees assessed against the agent. However, a credible argument can also be made that the award of fees arises out of the finding of fraud and therefore is not covered by the indemnity clause in the standard Independent Associate Agreement.

17

As pointed out earlier, the possibility of punitive damages also brings up a conflict of interest. Under statutory provisions, the broker can be liable for punitive damages because of the conduct of the agent only if the broker ratified or confirmed that conduct. Since the agent and broker are customarily joined as defendants in the litigation, the attorney representing them might not have a conflict until well into the trial when the question of punitive damages is raised. The astute agent at this point in the trial says: "Get me my own lawyer at your expense or hold me harmless from any punitive damages." Confronted with this choice in mid-trial, the broker, unless protected in the Independent Associate Agreement, probably has to agree to the indemnification. Even if the court were to permit a new lawyer to be brought in, the jury would wonder what was going on and the risk and expense would be staggering.

CAUTION ▷

Read and understand the agreement you have with your broker. Pay particular attention to that section dealing with "E & O" coverage. If coverage is not provided, and reasonably funded, it would be better to find another broker.

F. The Relationship Between Broker and Salesperson

18

Under the statutory scheme prevailing in California, real estate salespersons cannot receive compensation nor be employed by any person other than a broker holding their license at the time of the transaction.[30] The agent cannot even contract in his or her own name.[31] Conversely, the broker is under a duty to supervise the activities of the salesperson. In the event of a corporation, the responsible managing employee who has qualified the corporation for the license is the person responsible for the supervision of the salesperson. The duty of supervision extends beyond the requirement that the broker review and initial all material documents involved in transactions.[32] The broker is responsible for making certain the agent is properly advised of the various rules concerning conflict of interest, disclosure, and the required Standard of Care.

For example, in one case the broker permitted the agent to receive a credit for the broker's share of the commission because the agent was purchasing on his own account. Under these circumstances, the broker is obliged to make certain the seller of the property knows the agent is purchasing on his own account and not for a third person. Where it was called to the attention of the Department of Real Estate that the seller had not been so informed, the DRE instituted disciplinary proceedings against the broker, even though the seller had no complaints about the transaction. It concluded that since the broker authorized the disbursement of the broker's share of the commission back to the agent, the broker was aware of the transaction, had a duty to supervise the transaction, and an obligation to make certain the agent had informed the seller that the agent was participating as a principal.

It is the failure to supervise that most often leads to disciplinary proceedings against the broker. While the discipline imposed is usually relatively modest, 30 days' suspension for instance, even a temporary suspension can have a very severe effect on the broker's business. Publicity concerning disciplinary action also has an adverse effect.

The best way to control activities of the salesperson is to require the office file be fully documented and all required documents placed in the file on or before the close of escrow.

---

[30]Calif. Business & Professions Code §10137.

[31]*People v. Asuncion* (1984) 152 Cal.App.3d 422, 426; 199 Cal.Rptr. 514.

[32]The requirement of reviewing and initialling the document is found in the Real Estate Regulations, 10 Calif. Code of Regulations §2725(a).

Many brokers refuse to disburse a commission to the salesperson until the office file has been fully documented and those documents reviewed and approved by the broker. While the agent may find this annoying, it is completely justified from the broker's standpoint since the broker might otherwise be held liable and subject to disciplinary action for failure to supervise.

CAUTION ▶

Remember — for the purposes of establishing tort liability, that is, liability for negligence as well as intentional conduct, California courts hold, as a matter of law, that the broker is liable under the doctrine of *respondeat superior* ("let the master answer") for the acts of salespeople during the course and scope of the broker's business.[33] The rule is clearly set forth in the leading case of *Newcomb v. Title Guar. & Trust Co.*[34] where the court held that misrepresentations by the salesperson "are in law, the representations of the principal. Accordingly, where false and fraudulent representations are made by an agent in effecting a sale, the principal is equally responsible with the agent, although the latter had no intent to deceive the purchaser. . . So far as the purchaser is concerned, such representations have the same effect to bind the principal as though they were made by him in the first instance, and this is equally true whether they were made in his presence or absence."

19

In a recent case, a purchaser sued the mortgage loan broker and its salesperson for fraud because of the failure to timely fund a loan at the represented interest rate. After a court trial, a judgment for fraud was entered awarding general and punitive damages. Although the broker was held liable only under the doctrine of *respondeat superior*, the appellate court held that the Department of Real Estate could revoke the broker's license as well as that of the salesperson.[35]

RECOMMEND ▶

The result in this case seems very unfair. However, because of this potential for vicarious liability, the broker is well served by carefully screening potential agents before accepting them in the brokerage.

---

[33] *Grubb & Ellis Co. v. Spengler* (1983) 143 Cal.App.3d 890; 192 Cal.Rptr. 637.

[34] (1933) 131 Cal.App. 329, 332; 21 Pac.2d 456; 22 Pac.2d 552.

[35] *California Real Estate Loans, Inc. v. Wallace* (1993) 18 Cal.App.4th 1575; 23 Cal.Rptr.2d 462.

20

Part II

The Significance of "Standard of Care"

Like the physician treating a patient or the lawyer handling a probate, a real estate licensee is held to a standard of conduct and skill that conforms to that customarily practiced by similar professionals in the community. Courts look to statutory provisions to define this Standard of Care as well as regulations promulgated by the Department of Real Estate (including the Code of Professional Conduct[36]) and the Realtors® Code of Ethics. Sometimes the statute prescribes the particular Standard of Care applicable. For example, the conduct of an agent performing his or her duty to make a competent visual inspection is measured by the education, knowledge and experience required for the agent to obtain a license.[37]

The *Easton* case specifically held that expert testimony is ordinarily not required to establish the Standard of Care in the real estate industry or to determine whether an agent's conduct constitutes a breach of that standard.[38] Typically, however, the parties rely upon testimony from expert witnesses to establish whether the conduct of an agent in a particular situation is within the Standard of Care utilized by the ordinary agent practicing in the community. The designated expert usually reviews the documentation in a particular transaction, reads the depositions of the buyers, sellers and the agents, and then reaches a conclusion as to whether the conduct in question was within or outside of the Standard of Care. As one might expect, the outcome of a case rests, at least in part, on which expert the jury finds most persuasive. In any event, "Standard of Care" becomes a critical issue in most cases. In order to conduct himself or herself properly, the agent should have some basic understanding of the basis on which suit may

---

[36] 10 Calif. Code of Regulations, §2785.

[37] Calif. Civil Code §2079.2.

[38] *Easton v. Strassburger* (1986) 152 Cal.App.3d 90, 106; 199 Cal.Rptr. 383, 392-393.

be brought.

Unlike the areas of medical and legal malpractice, few attorneys specialize in lawsuits against real estate agents. Consequently, many plaintiffs' lawyers miss the more subtle ways in which liability can be imposed on the agent and the broker. For example, only recently have lawyers discovered that a broker's failure to adequately supervise an agent violates Department of Real Estate regulations and may lead to disciplinary action against the broker by the DRE. A violation of a regulation or statute requiring certain conduct constitutes negligence *per se*, that is, negligence as a matter of law, unless excused or justified. Failure to supervise often is readily established and, if the plaintiff obtains an instruction to the jury regarding negligence *per se*, a verdict for damages becomes a slam dunk.

However, the purpose of this manual is to assist agents and brokers and not act as a resource for litigious buyers or their attorneys![39] Consequently, the discussion is limited to the more conventional types of actions brought against agents and brokers.

22

A. Why Agents Are Sued

As with all wrongful conduct, actions against agents are divided into two categories — breach of contract actions and all other wrongful conduct actions, which are called "torts." Contract actions are created to enforce the intentions of the parties to the agreement. Tort law is primarily designed to vindicate social policy, that is, to make people pay damages for their wrongful acts.[40] In the context of real estate transactions, the tort causes of action consist of intentional misrepresentation, negligent misrepresentation, concealment, professional negligence, statutory negligence, and breach of fiduciary duty.

It is rare for the agent to be sued for breach of contract. Ordinarily, the agent is not a party to the purchase agreement. The agent and broker are parties to the listing agreement which provides that the agent will use his best efforts to market the property and find a purchaser. There is seldom any complaint

---

[39] In the winter of 1993, the California Continuing Education of the Bar published an Action Guide on "Approaching an Action Against a Real Estate Broker." One hopes such material will not encourage meritless litigation against brokers and agents.

[40] *Carma Developers (California), Inc. v. Marathon Development California, Inc.* (1992) 2 Cal.4th 342; 6 Cal.Rptr.2d 467.

that the agent has failed to fulfill this part of the bargain.

A few courts have taken the approach that there is also an implied contract[41] wherein the agent and broker will advise the parties skillfully, that the broker will supervise the activities of the agent, and the agent and broker will give professional advice to their principal throughout the negotiations. While the Statute of Frauds provides all contracts regarding the sale of real property must be in writing to be enforceable, there is an exception for fully executed contracts. A "fully executed contract" is one which has been completely performed by all the parties. Some courts hold this implied contract to represent the buyer and seller with skill is fully executed upon the close of escrow, and therefore outside the statute of frauds.

Almost all cases, however, will involve tort causes of action, that is, accusations that the agent and broker acted either fraudulently or negligently in the transaction. The nature of these causes of action can best be understood by examining the instructions that the jury is given when they are asked to find if the agent or broker is liable.

1. Fraud and Deceit

23

The first category of possible wrongful conduct for which an agent may be sued is generally labeled "fraud and deceit," which has three subcategories:

```
            FRAUD AND DECEIT

    Intentional              Negligent
  Misrepresentation       Misrepresentation

      Concealment
```

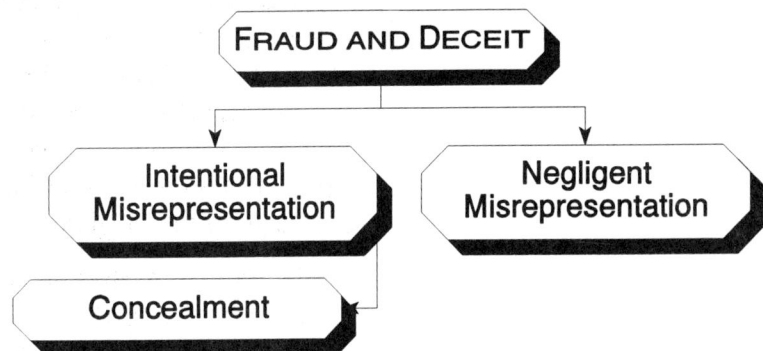

While some of the elements necessary to establish agent misconduct may seem complicated, remember these are the instructions given to the jury shortly before they retire to

---

[41] An "implied contract" is an agreement which may be established by the acts and conduct of the parties. *Peterson Development Co., Inc. v. Torrey Pines Bank* (1991) 233 Cal.App.3d 103; 284 Cal.Rptr. 367; Calif. Civil Code §1621.

deliberate. If you have difficulty absorbing this information, think how the juror who is going to decide your fate must feel when he or she is given in a few minutes what a law school student may study for a year. Little wonder the verdict is not always just.

Intentional Misrepresentation

In charging the jury as to **intentional misrepresentation**, the court will tell them:[42]

▶ (1) *The agent* must have made a representation as to a past or existing material fact;

▶ (2) The representation must be false;

▶ (3) *The agent* must have known that the representation was false when made or must have made the representation recklessly, without knowing whether it was true or false;

▶ (4) *The agent* must have made the representation with an intent to defraud the plaintiff, that is, the agent must have made the representation for the purpose of inducing the plaintiff to rely upon it and to act or to refrain from acting in reliance thereon;

▶ (5) *The plaintiff* (usually the buyer) must have been unaware of the falsity of the representation; must have acted in reliance upon the truth of the representation and must have been justified in relying upon the representation.

▶ (6) And, finally, as a result of the reliance upon the truth of the representation, *the plaintiff* must have sustained damage.

It is not often that the plaintiff is able to sustain the burden of proof and show the agent, as required under the third element, knew the representation was false. Occasionally, however, a jury finds the agent is lying and intentionally deceived the buyer regarding some aspect of the transaction. Under such circumstances, though the actual damages suffered by the buyer may be minimal, the possibility of punitive damages must be seriously considered. As pointed out later, however distasteful, preparation is necessary for this possibility.[43]

24

---

[42] 2 California Jury Instructions, Civil (1991 Revision) §12.31. This book of approved jury instructions is commonly referred to by the acronym BAJI, and is subsequently referred to as BAJI.

[43] See pp. 36-37, *infra.*

Concealment

The instruction for **concealment**, which by its nature is also an intentional tort, is usually as follows:[44]

▸ "(1) *The defendant agent* must have concealed or suppressed a material fact;

▸ "(2) *The defendant* must have been under a duty to disclose the fact to the plaintiff because either the defendant (a) was in a fiduciary relationship to the plaintiff, or (b) knew that the facts were neither known or readily accessible to the plaintiff;

▸ "(3) *The defendant* must have intentionally concealed or suppressed the fact with the intent to defraud the plaintiff;

▸ "(4) *The plaintiff* must have been unaware of the fact and would not have acted as he or she did if he or she had known of the concealed or suppressed fact;

▸ "(5) And, finally, as a result of the concealment or suppression of the fact, *the plaintiff* must have sustained damage."

Negligent Misrepresentation

For reasons never clearly explained, **negligent misrepresentation**, which does not involve intentional misconduct, is nevertheless categorized as "fraud and deceit" in California.[45] The elements of this cause of action are exactly the same as for intentional misrepresentation except for the third element. In negligent misrepresentation this element of the cause of action is:

▸ "(3) Regardless of the agent's actual belief, *the agent* must have made the representation without any reasonable ground for believing it to be true."[46]

A common example of negligent misrepresentation is when an agent purports to show the buyer the location of the boundary lines based on physical evidence such as trees or fences, when in fact the boundary line is located elsewhere. If the agent does not have a clue about boundary locations, a representation that they are located in a particular place might be so "reckless" as to constitute intentional fraud. It would certainly be a

25

---

[44]BAJI (Supp. 1993) §12.35.

[45]BAJI (Supp. 1993) §12.45. But in *Lacher v. Superior Court* (1991) 230 Cal.App.3d 1038; 281 Cal.Rptr. 640, the court said that fraud is an intentional tort and the element of fraudulent intent, or the intent to deceive, distinguishes it from negligent misrepresentation.

[46]BAJI §12.45 (1991 Revision).

negligent misrepresentation.

Other examples of representations which have been held negligent are: (a) statements that a psychiatric office can be operated out of a residence when in fact the zoning laws prohibit it; (b) the water supply from a well is adequate when it has not been professionally tested; (c) an attached second unit is legal when it has not been approved by the city; (d) an easement across adjoining property goes with the house when the easement is not appurtenant. The list is long. Agents should simply not make any representations in areas in which they are not qualified and should never make representations without verifying their accuracy.

2. Negligence

26

The negligence causes of action are the second group used to recover against brokers and agents. The law provides the agent must exercise the skill one would reasonably expect of a real estate salesperson who has special knowledge about real estate transactions. That is, the experience, training and education an agent needs to get a license. It is in the negligence causes of action that application of the "Standard of Care" is most commonly used.

Surprisingly, and certainly unrealistically, the law provides that an agent acting within the Standard of Care must have ordinary professional knowledge about:[47]

- title of the property;
- natural characteristics of the property;
- agency contracts;
- agreements of sale;
- deeds, mortgages, deeds of trust, bills of sale;
- land contracts;
- leases;
- principles of business and land economics;
- appraisals.

We all know the ordinarily skillful agent (and for that matter, the ordinary skillful broker) does not have a complete grasp of all these subjects. The courts, however, frequently assume the typical licensee has unlimited talent in any field involving real estate. Not surprisingly, the public perceives the agent is receiving $24,000 on the sale of a $400,000 home and should

---

[47]See Business & Professions Code §10153.

know what he or she is doing. Rarely does anyone consider commission splits or the fact that the agent normally winds up with two percent or less of the sale price for all the work done.

Causes of action for breach of this duty to perform within the Standard of Care can be divided into three categories:

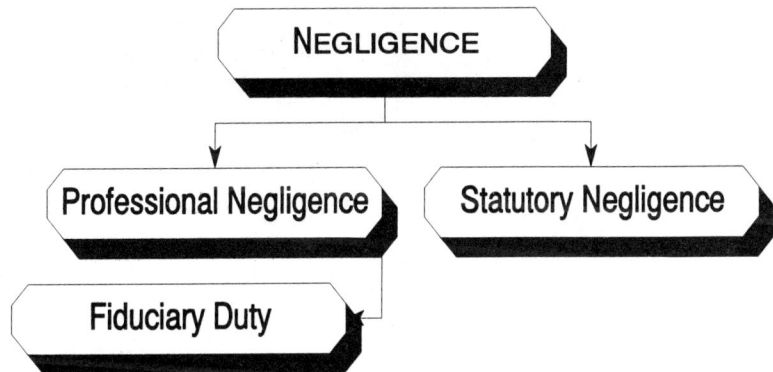

```
                    ┌─────────────────┐
                    │   NEGLIGENCE    │
                    └─────────────────┘
                       │           │
          ┌────────────┘           └────────────┐
          ▼                                     ▼
┌──────────────────────┐              ┌──────────────────────┐
│ Professional Negligence│            │ Statutory Negligence │
└──────────────────────┘              └──────────────────────┘
          │                                     ▲
          ▼                                     │
┌──────────────────────┐                        │
│    Fiduciary Duty    │────────────────────────┘
└──────────────────────┘
```

Professional Negligence

When instructing the jury on the elements of the cause of action for **professional negligence**, the court will charge them substantially as follows:[48]

"Defendant, as Plaintiff's real estate salesperson, had the duty to exercise reasonable skill and ordinary diligence in representing Plaintiff's interest. The skill required is that which you would reasonably expect of a real estate salesperson, who has special knowledge about real estate transactions. The knowledge required of Defendant includes ordinary professional knowledge about [here the court will insert some or all of the special skills set forth above]."

This instruction calls into play the "Standard of Care" concept. The question for the jury is whether the conduct of the agent was within the Standard of Care required of a similar professional practicing in a similar community.

Statutory Negligence

A violation of a statute or authorized regulation of a governmental entity can constitute **statutory negligence** unless compliance with the statute or regulation is prevented by some unusual circumstance. This is sometimes called **negligence per se.** Evidence Code section 669 sets forth the doctrine of negligence *per se* based on violation of a statute or regulation. That section provides in part: "(a) The failure of a person to exercise due care is presumed if (1) He violated a statute . . . ; (2) The violation

27

---

[48] 4 California Forms of Jury Instructions (1993 rev.) §62.30.

proximately caused . . . injury to . . . person or property; (3) The . . . injury resulted from an occurrence of the nature which the statute . . . was designed to protect; and (4) The person suffering the injury to his person or property was one of the class of persons for whose protection the statute was adopted. . . ." The first two elements are matters for the trier of fact and the second two are determined by the court as a matter of law.[49]

Although numerous statutes and regulations of the Department of Real Estate govern the conduct of real estate agents and brokers, the most frequently invoked are:

▶ (1) Civil Code §2374 — the statute providing for the disclosure form regarding agency relationships;

▶ (2) Civil Code §1102 — the property disclosure form;

▶ (3) Civil Code §2079 — the requirement of a visual inspection by both of the agents; and

▶ (4) Civil Code §2956 — disclosure of financing terms in transactions involving "seller financing."

The instruction the jury receives from the court regarding an alleged violation of these statutory provisions will be similar to the following:

▶ "If you find that defendant broker violated the statute or regulation just read to you, and that such violation was a cause of injury to plaintiff, you will find that such violation was negligence unless the defendant proves by a preponderance of the evidence that it did what might reasonably be expected of a person of ordinary prudence, acting under similar circumstances, who desired to comply with the law. In order to sustain such burden of proof, the defendant broker must prove by a preponderance of the evidence that it was faced with circumstances which prevented compliance or justified noncompliance with the statute or regulation."[50]

Since such violations would also be considered conduct below the Standard of Care, many plaintiffs' attorneys do not bother to ask for this additional instruction, fearful it will only confuse the jury. This can be a serious mistake on their part.

Sometimes the plaintiff alleges that failure to properly fill out and deliver the Agency Disclosure Form constitutes negligence *per se*. Until the adoption of Civil Code section 2374, consider-

----

[49]*Lua v. Southern Pacific Transportation Co.* (1992) 6 Cal.App.4th 1897, 1901; 9 Cal.Rptr.2d 116, 118.

[50]BAJI (1992 Revision) §3.45.

able confusion existed as to which of the principals in the transaction the licensee was representing. The prevailing theory was that if the property was placed on the multiple listing service, the selling agent (representing the buyer) was also the subagent of the seller and therefor a dual agent. Civil Code section 2374 spells out the various relationships, specifying under what circumstances the agent represents the buyer exclusively, the seller exclusively, or is a dual agent representing both. Because of the complexity of these agency relationships, preparation and delivery of the agency disclosure form is very important. Failure to comply with the statutory requirements can constitute negligence or lead to disciplinary proceedings.

Most litigation, however, deals with the property disclosure statement and the related duty of the agent to make a visual inspection of the premises. Because of their importance, these subjects are examined at length in Part III of this manual.

Breach of Fiduciary Duty

The last cause of action in the negligence group is called **breach of fiduciary duty**. It is well settled that both the agent and the broker owe a fiduciary duty to their principal. This duty is often compared to that of a trustee to its beneficiary.[51] The relationship imposes on the agent a requirement of loyalty, integrity, and good faith. Many writers conclude the relationship raises the ordinary Standard of Care in negligence actions to a higher level. An examination of the case law, however, indicates this is not true. Breach of fiduciary duty is a separate and distinct cause of action from negligence.

29

Where a fiduciary relationship exists, such as between the seller and the listing agent, the exposure of the agent is affected in several ways:

▶ A principal is ordinarily justified in relying on the advice of a fiduciary without making an independent investigation.

▶ The fiduciary has a duty to disclose all material facts which might affect the principal's decision (except the price the seller is willing to take and the buyer is willing to pay where there is a dual agency).

▶ Most important, the measure of damages recoverable by a plaintiff is not limited to the difference in value between

---

[51]See *Gann v. Williams Brothers Realty, Inc.* (1991) 231 Cal.App.3d 1698; 283 Cal.Rptr. 128, for an analysis of the rule that a real estate agent has the same obligation of undivided service and loyalty imposed on a trustee in favor of his beneficiary.

30

CAUTION

what he paid for and what he received (the "out of pocket" rule) as in fraud cases, but includes all losses caused by the alleged wrongful conduct, whether the harm or loss could be anticipated or not.[52]

Questions of breach of fiduciary duty arise not only in ordinary residential real estate transactions but in cases involving mortgage loan brokers governed by most, if not all, of the same rules as licensees in purchase and sale transactions. In the leading case of *Barry v. Raskov*,[53] the court held that a mortgage loan broker owes a fiduciary duty of good faith towards his principals, the lender-investor that puts money with the loan broker to place, and the borrower as well. This duty is non-delegable. Therefore the mortgage loan broker is responsible for the fraud or negligence of an independent property appraiser hired by the mortgage loan broker to appraise the property securing the loan. It makes no difference whether that appraiser is an agent of the mortgage loan broker or an independent contractor. In either situation the broker is responsible for his conduct.

The same kind of responsibility can be imposed on a broker or agent in residential transactions who retains, on behalf of one of the parties, an inspector or other professional to make a report on any of the physical conditions concerning the property. Remember, the buyer must retain these specialists. The agent should only make recommendations, and the recommendations should include at least three persons in each of the fields required. The recommendation list should also contain an exculpatory clause advising the buyer that the agent or broker bears no responsibility for the work to be performed.

---

[52]This peculiar result, which permits greater damages in negligence cases than is allowed in fraud cases, is discussed more fully at pages 34-35, *infra*.

[53](1991) 232 Cal.App.3d 447, 283 Cal.Rptr. 463.

B. How You Prove You Acted Within the Standard of Care

1. Documentation

CAUTION ▶

When a lawsuit is filed, the first thing the agent's attorney will do is review both the office file and the personal file of the agent involved. The more documentation contained in the file, the easier to accurately develop a picture of what happened. Agents often ask whether they should purify or otherwise clean up their file. The answer is a resounding NO! "Spoilation of evidence" is a crime as well as a civil tort. California Penal Code section 135 makes it a misdemeanor to willfully destroy or conceal physical evidence about to be produced in a trial or investigation authorized by law. Monetary damages can be awarded in a civil action for either negligent or intentional concealment or destruction of evidence.[54] Moreover, the evidence you destroy may be what you need to establish that you did act within the Standard of Care.

During the course of a trial, the best way of convincing a jury you are telling the truth is to have available records that can not only refresh your independent recollection, but are admissible themselves as business record entries made contemporaneously with the conduct in question. Such records are an exception to the hearsay rule which precludes the admission of certain types of evidence.

For example, at a recent trial the buyer testified at length that he first visited the property in question during an open house held on a Sunday. He distinctly remembered coming from church services and arriving at the house at 12:30 p.m. The defendant real estate agent was conducting the open house and allegedly, with a wave of her arm, told him the property included a heavily wooded area at the rear of the house. He walked around the property and left about 12:45. According to the buyer, he purchased the property relying heavily upon the representation of the agent as to the location of the property line. He was astounded to find out after close of escrow that the wooded area belonged to his back-yard neighbor. The loss of value to the property was "so great" that, aside from the severe emotional trauma he suffered, he sought damages for diminution in value of $150,000.

31

---

[54] The statute of limitation for spoilation of evidence is two years. *Augusta v. United Service Auto. Assn.* (1993) 13 Cal.App.4th 4; 16 Cal.Rptr.2d 400.

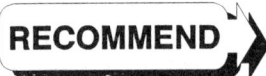

The agent could not even remember meeting the buyer, much less having a conversation about property lines at an open house, and she so testified at her deposition. Plaintiff's counsel, apparently never questioning the story of his client, failed to inquire whether any documentation supported the agent's whereabouts on the day in question. After her deposition, the agent managed to locate her diary, showing she had a luncheon scheduled with her manager on the day in question. The manager's calendar also showed the luncheon date for noon at a popular restaurant. He retrieved the Visa charge slip from storage, confirming the fact he did have lunch on the date in question with the agent.

During the trial, the buyer repeated his story about meeting the defendant at the open house at noon, embellishing his prior deposition testimony with considerable detail as to where and when he walked with the agent and the specifics of the conversations. When the documentary evidence was introduced by the defense, conclusively establishing that the agent was not even on the premises at the time plaintiff claimed, it was all over. The jury rendered a defense verdict after only two hours of deliberation. We will never know whether the plaintiff was confused on his dates or just lying. In any event, the documentation defeated him.

Many agents keep a calendar-type diary of their appointments, as well as a log on each transaction giving the date and time of significant telephone calls, visits to the property, inspections, problems that arise, and the position and conduct of each of the parties regarding those problems. When an attorney reviews an agent's file and sees such a log, an audible sigh of relief can be heard. At least the facts will be readily established since the log, **if the entries are made contemporaneously with the event**, is admissible in evidence. A log created some time after the fact does not have the same impact and is not usually admissible. Under some circumstances, however, even the after-the-fact log may be used to refresh a witness' memory.

32

RECOMMEND

2. Disclaimers

Disclaimers can be helpful. For example, they played an important part in a decision by the Court of Appeals arising out of a summary judgment granted in Yolo County in *Carleton v. Tortosa*.[55] The plaintiff employed a real estate broker to assist

---

[55] (1993) 14 Cal.App.4th 745; 17 Cal.Rptr.2d 734.

in the sale of two residential rental properties and the purchase of two similar properties. The transactions were not properly structured to qualify for a tax deferred exchange under Internal Revenue Code section 1031, and the investor sued the broker for professional negligence, claiming that the broker should have warned the plaintiff of possible adverse tax consequences.

The listing agreements, disclosure statements, and purchase contracts all contained disclaimers to the effect that real estate brokers do not give advice of tax or legal consequences of the transaction. The plaintiff argued these disclaimers were invalid because (1) they were simply boilerplate provisions she did not bother to read and (2) such exculpatory provisions are against the public policy in the State of California.

The court held the party's failure to read the documents does not permit that party to avoid their legal effect. The fact the disclaimers about giving tax advice were boilerplate did not make them a "contract of adhesion." A contract of adhesion is one where a standardized contract contains overreaching, unduly oppressive, and unconscionable provisions. The court found the disclaimers in this case were neither.

Regarding the public policy argument, the court looked to the statutory Agency Disclosure Statement required under Civil Code section 2375. This statute provides that the statement must contain the following language: "A real estate agent is a person qualified to advise about real estate. If legal or tax advice is desired, consult a competent professional." This, said the court, shows the public policy in California does not require real estate brokers to provide tax advice. **Make certain your contract of sale contains similar language**. (Current CAR, Coldwell Banker and Professional Publishing forms all contain this disclaimer.)

33

CAUTION ▶

The *Carlton* decision is another helpful case protecting real estate agents and indicates an apparent judicial trend limiting the Standard of Care required of brokers and agents. Nevertheless, care should be taken that the agent does not offer tax advice. Though the agent has no duty to advise with regard to the tax consequences of a transaction, once the agent puts his or her foot in the door, an obligation arises requiring the agent to make sure that the advice given is correct and reliable. Even with a disclaimer, an agent can be held liable for erroneous tax or legal advice. The safest course of action is to decline to give such advice and refer your clients to their attorney or accountant.

One well known commentator makes two interesting points regarding this case. First, if brokers do have a duty to give advice, they probably cannot protect themselves by a clause exculpating themselves for bad advice. Secondly, if disclaimers are to be used to legitimately limit the scope of the agent's responsibility to the principal, the disclaimer should be in the listing agreement and not in some document "midway through the deal when neither principal has any real opportunity to protest."[56]

As a practical matter, agents have little input into exculpatory language in standard preprinted forms. Adding language, other than the common provisions regarding boundaries and like matters, would certainly evoke suspicion in the mind of the principal. While agents should be aware of the implication of disclaimers, their best course of action is not to give advice or make any representations regarding fields where they have no expertise or obligation to give advice.

RECOMMEND

C. Possible Exposure

34

Failure to adhere to the Standard of Care, whether negligent or intentional, can result in substantial monetary damages. To good producers, the threat of license revocation is even more threatening. These results, and minimizing their impact, are briefly discussed in the following pages.

1. Money Damages

The damages that can be awarded for breach of contract are the broad "benefit of the bargain" measure of damages, which compensate the plaintiff for all harm that might follow from the breach.[57] Agents, however, are seldom sued for breach of contract. Most often, actions against agents are for fraud, professional negligence, or breach of fiduciary duty. The damages recoverable by a plaintiff for the fraud of the broker or agent, including intentional or negligent misrepresentation, oddly enough, are more limited than damages recoverable for breach of contract. Civil Code section 3343 specifies that in actions for fraud in the purchase, sale, or exchange of real property, plaintiffs are limited to recovering their "out-of-pocket" losses. This means the difference between what the buyer paid for the

---

[56]Bernhardt, CEB Real Property Law Reporter (July 1993) p. 232.

[57]Calif. Civil Code §3300 provides: ". . . the measure of damages . . . is the amount which will compensate the party aggrieved for all the detriment proximately caused [by the breach of contract], or which, in the ordinary course of things, would be likely to result therefrom."

property and its value at the time of purchase.[58] Consequently, even if the agent is found guilty of failing to reveal some defect, plaintiffs cannot recover if the fair market value of the property at the time of sale was equal to or greater than what the buyers paid for it. This is true even if the buyers would not have bought the property if they had known the truth.[59]

Recoverable damages become even more complicated if the agent and the plaintiff are in a fiduciary relationship, such as the seller and the listing agent, or the buyer and the selling agent. Under such circumstances, the courts hold the limiting measure of damages for fraud does not apply, and the broader benefit of the bargain measure of damages is proper. That is, where breach of a fiduciary relationship is alleged, the buyer can claim that had the property been as represented, its value would have been greater than its actual value, and they are entitled to the difference. But in order to invoke this broader measure of damages, buyers must prove the agent acted dishonestly, i.e., breached the agent's fiduciary duty. Ordinary negligence claims should not give rise to this benefit of the bargain measure of damages.[60]

Some parties sue agents for damages due to "emotional distress" they claim to have suffered. Fortunately, more recent decisions hold that unless the conduct of the accused party is so outrageous that severe distress to the plaintiff should have been foreseen, damages for stress are not recoverable. As one court noted, "Litigation is frequently stressful and disagreeable, even when one is a plaintiff."[61]

Regardless of which measure of damages applies, most broker-agent agreements provide that the broker will indemnify the agent from either the cost of defending or judgments resulting from such a claim. Sometimes an agent is liable for a relatively modest deductible amount or, more often, shares the

35

---

[58]Calif. Civil Code §3343(a)(1)-(4) also allows the plaintiff to recover damages for loss of profits, loss of use and certain incidental expenses.

[59]Rescission, that is, cancelling the sale, might still be an available option to the defrauded buyer. However, if the property has increased in value, the buyer will not likely utilize this remedy.

[60]For an excellent analysis of these complicated distinctions, often misunderstood by trial judges, see O'Leary, *Limiting the Fiduciary Duty Exception to the Out-of-Pocket Rule* (April 1993) 16 CEB Real Property Law Reporter 145.

[61]*Pleasant v. Celli* (1993) 18 Cal.App.4th 841; 22 Cal.Rptr.2d 663, 670. But emotional distress damages have been awarded against a builder/seller where defective construction caused water problems. *Salka v. Dean Homes of Beverly Hills, Inc.* (1993) 18 Cal.App.4th 1145; 22 Cal.Rptr.2d 902.

cost of the defense with the broker up to a specified amount. Even with an allegation of intentional concealment or misrepresentation, the broker, as a practical matter, is usually responsible for any damages unless the amount of the damage attributable to the intentional misconduct of the agent is clearly segregated in the jury verdict or the court's statement of decision.

However, if the jury finds, **by clear and convincing evidence**,[62] that the agent was guilty of "fraud, oppression or malice", it may award punitive damages.[63] The broker is not liable for punitive damages unless it authorized or ratified the agent's misconduct.[64] If punitive damages appear possible, do not be surprised if the attorney hired by the broker (although ostensibly representing the agent) appears to be insulating the broker from responsibility for the agent's conduct. A real and substantial conflict of interest can develop at this point since the broker's interest is to let the guilty agent "swing in the wind" and for the broker to distance itself from any liability. It must be remembered the broker has no obligation to indemnify the agent from an award of punitive damages.

CAUTION ▷

Normally determining the extent of punitive damages is the function of a separate mini-trial. During the first phase of the trial, the jury is asked whether the agent or broker was guilty of fraud, oppression, or malice. Some judges also ask the jury whether, in such event, punitive damages should be awarded — but not the amount. If the jury answers "yes" to both questions, a recess is taken and the second phase of the trial begins. Evidence is presented as to the amount to be awarded. Jurors are seldom told the first time they are instructed that they will have to hear additional evidence and retire to again deliberate if they find the agent liable for punitive damages.

During this second phase of the trial, evidence is introduced as to the agent's net worth and income. If the jury finds the broker ratified the conduct, evidence of the broker's net worth is also introduced. Based on this information, the jury is instructed that they should assess damages against the defendants sufficient to punish them and deter any repetition of the offensive conduct. In the case of *Storage Services v. Osterbaun*,[65] the court suggested the appropriate amount of punitive damages

36

---

[62]The standard ordinarily used to assess liability is the lower standard of "preponderance of the evidence."

[63]Calif. Civil Code §3294 (a), (c).

[64]Calif. Civil Code §3294 (b).

[65](1989) 214 Cal.App.3d 498; 262 Cal.Rptr. 689

might be ten percent of the agent's net worth. Such a rule, however, has never been formally established. Punitive damage awards against an agent in the $50,000 range are not uncommon.

Such an award is normally devastating to the agent. Worse, the law also provides that in such a case the DRE has the authority to revoke the agent's license. Even though the law requires "clear and convincing" evidence to support an award of punitive damages, in some cases the agent simply is not as persuasive as his or her antagonist before the jury. It is especially heartbreaking where the award is made on a split jury vote — only nine of the twelve are necessary to render a verdict. In one conversation with jurors following such a verdict, it was clear the three dissenting jurors did not believe the agent liable at all, and some on the majority were still ambivalent about who was telling the truth. Jurors do not always listen to or understand the instructions. A hidden prejudice against real estate agents and brokers is often not evident during the jury selection process; and it is often shocking to learn the basis for their decision. Justice is not always served.

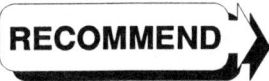

RECOMMEND

While most professions entail some risk of liability, real estate agents should be particularly aware of their exposure to punitive damages. Adequate record keeping and, when in doubt, supervision from the responsible manager or broker are the agent's best protection.

37

2. License Revocation or Suspension

The Real Estate Commissioner has broad powers to cite licensees for misconduct and, after a hearing before an administrative hearing officer, can suspend or revoke a license. While the hearing enables a licensee, or his counsel, to present evidence either denying the allegations or in mitigation, the proceedings are substantially slanted in favor of disciplinary action. The hearing officer makes recommendations to the Real Estate Commissioner and, in most cases, they are followed. The Commissioner issues the order suspending or revoking the license. One year later the licensee can petition the Department of Real Estate for reconsideration or reinstatement of the license.

For minor infractions the license is usually suspended for a period of time, or the licensee is given a restricted license requiring substantially greater broker supervision than under ordinary circumstances. Where there is financial misconduct, such as appropriation of a client's funds, revocation of the license almost always ensues.

Failure to Supervise

The broker as well as the agent is subject to disciplinary proceedings for violating regulations. A common accusation against the broker is failure to supervise the licensee's activities as required by Business and Professions Code section 10177(h). Whenever the agent is disciplined, the Department of Real Estate almost always looks to see if the brokers's conduct was appropriate. Failure to adequately supervise usually leads to a suspension of the license for a period of time. But the suspension is often stayed if the infraction is not serious and there is no willful wrongdoing on the broker's part.

Misconduct is most often called to the attention of the Department of Real Estate by parties to a real estate transaction. The proceedings before the Department of Real Estate are quasi-criminal in nature so if a disgruntled party to a real estate transaction threatens an agent — "pay me or I'll complain to the DRE" — he or she may be guilty of extortion. In many cases, however, the disgruntled party, usually a buyer, is usually so angry he or she uses every means at his or her disposal to punish or seek retribution from the licensee, including filing a complaint. Sometimes this is done because the purchaser does not feel he or she has sufficient funds to proceed with civil litigation and believes that filing a complaint with the Department of Real Estate will afford financial redress. However, the Department of Real Estate is not a collection agency. It cannot compel a licensee to pay damages to an aggrieved party to a purchase agreement.

Failure to Reveal Participation

Sometimes filing a complaint with the Department of Real Estate can cause a complainant more grief than anticipated. For example, in one case a manager, also a licensed broker, decided he would like to live in and be a part owner (one way or the other) of a residential property he had listed for sale. He approached former clients and worked out an oral equity share arrangement with them. As the listing agent he would credit his commission towards the purchase price; then his clients would use their credit to get a loan and take title in their own names. The listing agent would live in the house and pay the mortgage payment in lieu of rent. Profits on resale would be split equally. To make certain the loan and the commission would be sufficient to cover the purchase price, the parties agreed the seller would credit the buyer with $25,000 of "non-recurring closing costs," thereby inflating the purchase price to obtain a higher loan. The buyers also indicated on their loan application that they were going to occupy the property to qualify for a

38

lower rate. The seller did not know the listing agent was going to be a silent part-owner, but he later indicated he could have cared less since he obtained the price which he wanted.

After the sale closed, the buyers both obtained broker's licenses, primarily because of their frequent real estate dealings. The listing agent moved into the property and all appeared to be going well. But then the occupying agent got behind in his mortgage payments and failed to tell the buyers about his problem. The buyers were furious when they had to make up the delinquent payments and resell the property, "according to them," at a loss. The buyers filed a complaint with the Sonoma County Board of Realtors claiming that the occupying agent had breached his fiduciary duty by not making the mortgage payments in a timely fashion. The Sonoma Board, recognizing this case involved complexities beyond its ability to solve within its limited resources, declined to hear the matter. It also concluded that questions of whether the agent failed to make timely payments had nothing to do with the ethics of the transaction, which was all they were concerned about.

When the Sonoma Board failed to hear the matter, the buyers filed a complaint with the Department of Real Estate, claiming the DRE should help them get their money back from the agent and his supervising broker. Quite understandably, the Department of Real Estate had no interest in whether the agent made his payments on time. It was interested, however, in the fact the agent did not tell the seller he was going to be an equity partner in the deal, and his commission was going to be part of the down payment. The Department filed accusations and held a hearing. The agent's license was revoked and his broker of record reprimanded for not adequately supervising the errant agent. The broker received a 30-day suspension which was stayed, that is, not enforced providing the supervising broker had no further infractions for a period of one year.

39

Turning to the buyers, the DRE found, despite the fact that the local loan officer was aware of the deal, that failing to reveal all the facts on the loan application "was both serious and blatant and warrants severe discipline." It proceeded to revoke the licenses of both of the buyers — the original complainants. Talk about being hoisted on one's own petard!

The lessons from this case are clear. You never know when, for some off-the-wall reason, one of your transactions is going to be reviewed in depth by the Department of Real Estate. The guidelines and regulations of the DRE are relatively brief and usually understandable. Though it may take a little more time, take care to stay within the confines of these regulations. In the

CAUTION

case at hand there was no reason the agent could not have told the seller he was going to be a part owner in the property and received the seller's consent. Very little effort would have saved considerable grief on all sides.

Kickbacks

On occasion, the basis for disciplinary action arises out of conduct on the part of the licensee which is in violation of the Real Estate Settlement Procedures Act of 1974, commonly referred to as RESPA. This act outlines certain disclosures and procedures which must be followed in any real estate transaction which involves "a federally related mortgage loan." Practically speaking, this involves almost all real estate transactions. Among other prohibitions, the act provides that there shall be no kickbacks or payments of anything of value to persons in a real estate transaction for referrals unless they are licensees.

It is most common for licensees, as a part of their promotional effort, to offer third parties money or gifts for client referrals, whether they be sellers or buyers. For example, one licensee did a clever promotion by sending out an enlarged copy of a $500 bill with her picture in the center and the promise that the recipient could turn the certificate into real money by simply referring a seller or buyer to her; they would be paid at the close of escrow. This violates the provisions of 12 USC §2607(a) and 24 CFR §3500.14(f) which preclude the giving of kickbacks. While paying fees to finders is permissible under California law, it is prohibited under the federal statute.

It is also common to see advertisements from well known brokers and agents promising "FINDER'S FEE PAID." This too, is a clear violation of the law.

The anti-kickback provisions of RESPA were adopted because of the prevailing practice of lenders and title companies to pay referral fees, thereby increasing the cost of services provided. Although perhaps not intended by the drafters of the legislation, the language clearly prohibits the payment of a referral fee to an unlicensed person.

While giving gratuities to finders in real estate transactions is not usually pressed, if some promotional piece offering gratuities falls into the hands of someone from the Department of Real Estate or a federal agency, the agent risks disciplinary proceedings.

Another rule in connection with RESPA is that the agent cannot insist on using any particular title company. The selecting of the title company is solely the role of the purchaser paying the title insurance premium. The law even precludes the seller from insisting upon naming the title company.

40

Misrepresentations

Other conduct commonly giving rise to disciplinary action includes making false or misleading advertisements and any representation concerning the property (such as its size, boundary lines, or square footage) without a reasonable basis for believing it to be true.

Whenever a court or jury finds an agent guilty of intentional fraud in a transaction, particularly where punitive damages have been awarded, the Department of Real Estate is charged with holding disciplinary hearings to determine whether or not his or her license should be revoked or other discipline imposed. The finding of fraud by a jury or court is conclusive, and it is very difficult to avoid revocation of a license on this ground. While the DRE does not seek these verdicts from local court records, they are often made aware of the finding of the court or jury by notification from the prevailing party. The only thing a licensee can do under such circumstances is to present mitigating evidence to attempt to obtain a restricted license rather than a revocation. The chances of success, however, are slim.

Once a trial court or jury finds an agent guilty of misconduct, the parties cannot stipulate that the judgment be set aside so as to avoid disciplinary proceedings. The appellate court held that to permit the offending agent to buy his or her way out of an adverse judgment "would undercut the authority of a state agency to regulate and discipline real estate licensees."[66]

41

Appeals

Sometimes the Department of Real Estate gets carried away with disciplinary action. Under these circumstances, if the licensee feels unjustly disciplined, he or she can seek redress by filing a petition to review the action in the Superior Court. This is called a petition for a writ of *mandamus*, that is, a request for an order compelling the DRE to reverse its decision. In the case of *Vaill v. Edmonds*,[67] the court reversed a DRE decision revoking a real estate broker's license for failure to warn property buyers of geological hazards on the property. The court found substantial evidence supporting the trial court's findings that the broker was neither negligent nor incompetent with regard to her advice conveying information of hazards to the buyer. The broker had told the buyers there existed a water problem with the property because of previous landslide activity, and the sellers had disclosed erosion problems on the property. Previous

---

[66]*Norman L. Krug Real Estate Investments, Inc. v. Praszker* (1993) 20 Cal.App.4th 226; 24 Cal.Rptr.2d 632 (rehearing granted December 21, 1993).

[67](1991) 4 Cal.App.4th 247; 6 Cal.Rptr.2d 1.

RECOMMEND

difficulties regarding ground water and landslide problems were disclosed. According to the court this was sufficient disclosure on the part of the agent, so there was no basis for license revocation.

Qualified counsel should always be consulted when an accusation is filed.

42

Part III

The Property Disclosure Statement

A. Importance of The Statement

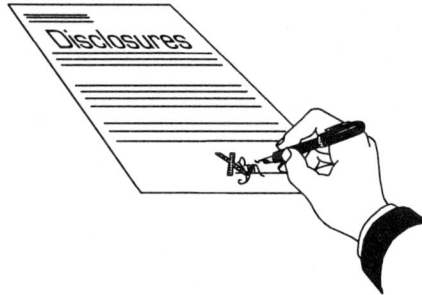

The decision in *Easton v. Strassburger*[68] led to the requirement that agents representing both buyer and seller make a competent **visual inspection** of the property and report to the buyer any facts materially affecting the property. A year later California adopted laws requiring the seller to disclose in writing any defects in their property.[69] The law in California and at least six other states[70] was passed at the behest of the National Association of Realtors to give protection to agents from liability for undisclosed defects.

It is expected an additional twenty states will require property disclosure statements within the next few years. Most other states have voluntary disclosure forms which are often required by real estate brokers.

While a few brokers complain most of the litigation confronting them concerns the disclosure statement, it is generally agreed the use of the statement has greatly reduced litigation and agent exposure. In almost any trial brought against brokers and their agents, a blown-up version of the disclosure statement can be seen on the courtroom exhibit board. Since the most frequent complaint is failure to disclose, no wonder the disclosure statement sits center stage in most real estate litigation.

From a risk management standpoint, the **transfer disclosure statement** has assumed more significance than the contract of sale itself. The care to be given to completing the transfer disclosure statement cannot be exaggerated. If both seller and

43

---

[68](1984) 152 Cal.App.3d 90; 199 Cal.Rptr. 383.

[69]Calif. Civil Code §1102 *et seq.*

[70]Disclosure statements are also required in Kentucky, Maine, New Hampshire, Oregon, Virginia and Wisconsin.

listing agent take the time to fill it out properly, considerable controversy and misunderstanding can be avoided. Your motto should be "Better to reveal than conceal."

The Transfer Disclosure Statement is not required in commercial transactions, foreclosure sales, probate sales, subdivisions where there is a public report (DRE "white slip"), and certain other listed transactions.[71] However, in *Karoutas v. HomeFed Bank* [72]the court imposed on beneficiaries and trustees in foreclosure proceedings the common law duty to disclose known conditions. In an apparent attempt to modify this case, the legislature amended Civil Code section 2924h(g) to permit foreclosure property to be sold "as is." However, the seller cannot escape liability for failing to disclose known conditions even in an "as is" sale. Sophisticated buyers require a disclosure statement in commercial transactions regardless of whether the property is being sold "as is."

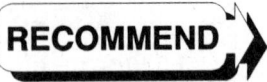

RECOMMEND

44

B. Basic Rules for Filling out the Statement

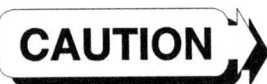

CAUTION

The best time to complete the statement is when taking the listing. Sit down with the sellers and fill out the form together so any questions they might have can be readily answered. The cardinal rule is **the agent never fills out the transfer disclosure statement in his or her own handwriting**. While letting the agent fill out the form may seem an expeditious way to complete the task, if there is an error on the part of the seller, either negligent or intentional, the seller will invariably testify at trial that the agent was told the proper response but failed to record it correctly on the TDS. This defense can hardly be raised if the answer is in the seller's own handwriting. Of course, extraordinary circumstances such as infirmity or other disability may preclude the seller from filling out the statement. In such event, that fact should be noted on the statement itself so there can be no later misunderstanding.

It is below the Standard of Care simply to hand the TDS forms to the sellers and tell them you will be back to pick them up when they have been completed. While there is nothing improper in letting the sellers review the forms before they are

---

[71]Calif. Civil Code §1102.1.

[72](1991) 232 Cal.App.3d 767; 283 Cal.Rtpr. 809.

filled out, it is inexcusable not to **review each question** with them making certain they understand the questions and answer them accurately. Even the most sophisticated seller will appreciate this concern on the agent's part.

The statement must be filled out and delivered to a prospective purchaser as soon as practicable before the transfer of title.

1. Sections I and II

Sections I and II of the TDS are directed to the seller. The law provides that the seller's duty to disclose does not relieve the prospective buyer of the duty to exercise reasonable care to protect himself or herself, discerning facts within the diligent attention and observation of a prospective buyer.[73] However, a buyer's inspection is not a defense to an action against a seller based on failure to disclose defects when the defective conditions are not visible and known only to the seller.[74]

In filling out the TDS the seller is obliged to reveal all material defects in the property. Whether information has sufficient materiality to affect the value or desirability of the property is a question of fact. The court or jury may make this determination based on its own knowledge or experience or rely upon expert testimony. **The test of materiality is whether the "negative fact" can reasonably be said to have a foreseeable depressing effect on the value of the property**.

In *Alexander v. McKnight,*[75] the seller failed to disclose that his neighbors engaged in a pattern of offensive and noxious activities, that is, they were party animals. The court said a seller cannot make an implied representation to a potential buyer "that the neighborhood is, and has been, an oasis of tranquility in an otherwise oppressive urban environment." Therefore, the existence of obnoxious neighbors that are a constant source of irritation must be disclosed.

Given this liberal interpretation of what must be disclosed to potential buyers under Civil Code section 1102.6, sellers should

45

---

[73]Calif. Civil Code §2079 *et. seq.*

[74]*Karoutas v. HomeFed Bank* (1991) 232 Cal.App.3d 767; 283 Cal.Rptr. 809.

[75](1992) 7 Cal.App.4th 973; 9 Cal.Rptr.2d 453.

CAUTION

RECOMMEND

46   **2. Sections III and IV**

be cautioned that **every negative factor should be disclosed**.

Sellers often ask their agent whether they should disclose defective conditions that have been repaired. More often than not, the agent, anxious to present to potential buyers a clean TDS, advises the seller to omit such information. However, many homeowners are "do it yourselfers," and the repairs are not up to code or are not a permanent solution. Electrical repairs seem to fascinate homeowners, who do not have a clue about building code requirements. Drainage problems are almost always "solved" without consulting an engineer. These repairs seem adequate, particularly during drought periods, but the first big storm can demonstrate the limitation of home-grown solutions!

Where, during the sellers' occupancy, roof leaks have been repaired, drains installed, or other similar repairs made, they should be noted on the transfer disclosure statement, together with the date they were made.

Under Civil Code section 2079, both the listing and the selling real estate agents must conduct a "reasonably competent and diligent **visual inspection**" of the property offered for sale. Sections III and IV of the TDS are the places where the respective agents report the results of their inspections.

Despite all the writings and decisions on the point, the law is still not clear how far agents, as distinguished from sellers, must go in their inspection. In the case of *Wilson v. Century 21 Great Western Realty*,[76] the court seemed to indicate the duty of the agents is limited to problems regarding the "sold property." It relieved brokers of liability for a defective foundation not readily observable, despite the fact that a neighbor told the agent he knew other properties in the area had foundation problems. The attorney representing the defendant brokers in that case notes, "If subsequent courts adopt this language . . . and limit a broker's duties of disclosure and investigation to the subject property, then brokers would be relieved of the duty to disclose items such as the presence of a commune or a battered

---

[76](1993) 15 Cal.App.4th 298; 18 Cal.Rptr.2d 779.

women's shelter in the neighborhood, the presence of noisy or criminal neighbors, and the like."[77]

Until a definitive opinion is rendered, the better course of action is to disclose all matters that a reasonable inspection of the area, including the specific property, would reveal; provided, of course, that such matters could materially affect the value of the property.

Since only a "visual" inspection is required, this might seem trivial. But remember, the "visual" inspection is a statutory requirement. There is also the common law requirement that an agent act within the Standard of Care required of similarly situated professionals. This may require more than a visual inspection. Exactly what is required is not always clear, and expert witnesses often disagree in trial testimony as to what conduct is within the Standard of Care.

RECOMMEND

At a minimum, the agent should conduct a walk-through of each room in the interior of the house as well as the outside area. Particular care should be taken to note evidence of any of the recurring disclosure problems discussed in detail beginning at page 59, *infra*. Pre-printed check lists suggesting what to look for are very helpful. Professional Publishing's "Red Flag Checklist" sets forth a comprehensive list of possible defects. Such a checklist can be incorporated by reference into the agents' section of the TDS by saying "See checklist attached," or similar language.

47

If a checklist is not incorporated, the comments by the agent should be straightforward. "There are water stains on the ceiling in the bedroom." "The building department cannot locate a permit for the family-room addition." Do not include the familiar disclaimer "Agent is not a licensed contractor and has no such skill." Such disclaimers are a waste of time.

CAUTION

Be careful not to adopt the statements of the seller. "I agree with everything the seller has disclosed," can become a trap. This, in effect, states that you have adopted the disclosures of the seller. If the seller has been untruthful or careless in making disclosures, you could be charged with the same misconduct. The TDS provides the "representations made by the sellers . . . are not the representations of the agents. . . ." Keep them that way!

---

[77]O'Leary, 16 CEB Real Property Law Reporter (July 1993) pp. 233-234.

"I can find nothing other than disclosed by the seller," is another typical statement made in the agents' section of the TDS. The agents' visual inspection should be independent from that of the seller. There is nothing wrong with noting defects that are visually apparent even though they have also been disclosed by the seller. The best course of action is to use an inspection checklist and incorporate it by reference in the TDS.

C. Supplemental Disclosure Statements

48

Some brokers, with an abundance of caution, have developed their own "supplemental disclosure statement." These can be very elaborate — while others contain only a few items, usually referring to special conditions prevailing in the community which the buyer may wish to know. Like the primary Transfer Disclosure Statement, the supplemental statement is not a part of the contract. As stated in the statutory form, "THIS INFORMATION IS A DISCLOSURE AND IS NOT INTENDED TO BE PART OF ANY CONTRACT BETWEEN THE BUYER AND SELLER." This is because the disclosure statement is not a contractual promise or warranty — it is simply a statement concerning the condition of the property being sold.

This distinction was illustrated in the recent case of *Brasier v. Sparks*.[78] There the plaintiff argued the seller was guilty of breach of contract because the Transfer Disclosure Statement said the seller was unaware of any building code violations; in fact several such code violations existed. The court held the disclosure statement cannot be relied upon as a part of the purchase contract or as a separate contract containing conditions upon which the primary purchase agreement is based. **Failure to disclose does not constitute a breach of contract**, which would have entitled the buyer to a broad range of damages.[79] Under tort liability, i.e., concealment, the buyer is only entitled to the difference in value between what he got and what he paid. Since the plaintiff could not prove the property was worth

---

[78](1993) 17 Cal.App.4th 1756; 22 Cal.Rptr.2d 1.

[79]The damage recoverable for breach of contract is that amount which will compensate the injured party for all loss caused by the breach, or which, in the ordinary course of things, would be likely to result from the breach. BAJI §10.90 (1992 Revision).

less than he paid, the court did not even have to decide whether the seller was guilty of fraud.

The author recently received a sample statement prepared by a large brokerage labeled "Addendum C" which stated "This Addendum is made a part of the Real Estate Purchase Agreement" and "This Document is Part of a Legally Binding Contract." An examination of the "addendum" revealed it contained, in part, modifications to the purchase agreement which properly belong in an addendum. However, a substantial part of the addendum was in fact a supplemental disclosure statement not intended to be a part of the contract. Such a document can create a trap for the unwary seller and possibly the agents involved. It can change a disclosure of a condition into some sort of promise and, to the extent the agents participate in making these "disclosures," they can become parties to the contract with all the attendant liabilities! **It is much easier for a purchaser to prove the seller breached the contract than it is to prove there was an intentional or negligent misrepresentation as to the condition of the property**. In addition, comparative negligence (whereby the fault, if any, on the part of the buyer reduces the seller's damages proportionately) is not available to reduce the seller's exposure in breach of contract cases. Finally, breach of contract might give rise to damages not available in tort causes of action.

49

If using a disclosure statement in addition to the statutory form, label it "**SUPPLEMENTAL DISCLOSURE STATEMENT**" and, like the statutory form, specifically state:

RECOMMEND

THIS INFORMATION IS IN ADDITION TO THE STATUTORY FORM AND NOT INTENDED TO BE PART OF ANY CONTRACT BETWEEN THE BUYER AND SELLER

One large brokerage employs a supplemental disclosure statement three legal-sized pages in length containing 37 questions! Some of the questions are compound and could easily catch a seller and the seller's agent. For example, the form asks "Does this property or any property within a two block radius have a high water table?" If, as one would suspect, the seller has not a clue about the water table on property two blocks away, the proper answer is "No" as to "this property," and "Unknown" as to property two blocks away. The form does not give this option, so the agent must modify the form to correctly express the knowledge of the seller. **Do not let the form control your response. Change it if necessary**.

Another brokerage uses a supplemental disclosure form stating it "is not intended to be and is not considered by me to be a representation of the physical condition of the property." This is a foolish disclaimer. Of course when you answer "good" to the question of "What is the condition of the garage door opener," you are making a representation as to the condition of the property. The seller is only going to be embarrassed when confronted by such language on cross-examination.

Whenever possible, stick with the statutory form and avoid supplemental disclosure statements, unless they contain pre-printed information that is applicable to the particular area. Asking questions such as whether the seller thinks there are "conditions in the neighborhood which make the area undesirable" call for subjective speculation which only gives the buyer an excuse for subsequent misrepresentation claims. After all, the seller is not guaranteeing that the buyer will find nirvana.

Elaborate supplemental disclosure statements prepared by some brokers seem designed to protect the broker without giving much thought to the fact the seller is being unjustifiably exposed.

CAUTION

50

1. Septic Systems

A substantial number of disputes reaching litigation involve failing septic systems. Apparently most agents do not think disclosures regarding septic systems are important because in the past, installation and repair of septic systems involved only minimal expenditure. The case today is most different. Because of environmental health requirements, systems must be professionally designed and often cost $20,000 to $30,000 to install. In some cases, newly enacted ordinances are so strict that specially designed above-surface "mound" systems must be utilized. In other cases, a lot is found unsuitable for any expansion of an existing system, thus prohibiting additions or modifications to the residence. This can lead to substantial claims for fraud and misrepresentation against both the seller and the agents. Again, attorney's fees can play an important role. While their recovery in tort (as distinguished from breach of contract) cases may be disputed, attorney's fees can be substantial.

In one case, settled on the eve of trial, the purchaser was paid $92,500 by the seller, the agents involved, and the septic tank inspection company. $30,000 of this amount was for a new system, with the balance for attorney fees and costs incurred in prosecuting the action. The inspection company was included because it inspected only the tank and not the leach lines which were found to be leaking. The agents were held responsible because they recommended the inspector and failed to advise the purchaser to have a complete inspection.

Often septic inspections consist of nothing more than pumping out the tank and taking a look at the tank to see whether it appears to be functioning properly. A proper inspection includes pressure testing the leach lines to see if they are operational. As with all inspections, the agent must be careful to give the prospective purchaser at least three names of available inspectors and be certain the purchaser is made aware that he or she, and not the agent, is selecting the inspector.

In one case the agent advised the buyer against having the septic system tested because it had been recently replaced. Two years after escrow closed, the purchaser noticed a leak in a leach line. It turned out that, unbeknownst to both the seller and his agent, the replacement did not include the defective leach line. The leach line could not be repaired because by then the city required any property on a failing septic system to hook up to a newly installed sewer system. The cost of the hookup, which included obtaining an easement from a blackmailing neighbor, was substantial. After mediation, the defendants contributed to a settlement — the seller $6,000; the listing agent $5,250; the selling agent $1,250; and the contractor who replaced the system $6,250. **Septic inspections should be performed in all cases**, regardless of when the system was installed.

CAUTION ▷

While no one wants to add to the paperwork associated with a sale, it is highly recommended that a special disclosure statement be given and explained to each purchaser of a residence having a septic system. Appendix A contains a septic tank disclosure form which should substantially reduce exposure in the septic tank area, particularly if agents explain the form to prospective purchasers rather than merely handing it to them.[80]

RECOMMEND ▷

51

2. Seller Financing

When seller carry-back financing was popular, buyers often were misinformed as to the exact nature of the loans they were

---

[80]A generic version of this form is available from Professional Publishing, 122 Paul Drive, San Rafael, CA 94903 (Telephone 800-288-2006), Form No. 110.70.

assuming in connection with the transaction. Sellers were confused about the creative financing being used. Deals frequently were structured putting sellers in danger of losing their equity.

To help remedy this situation, the legislature enacted Civil Code sections 2956-2967, effective July 1, 1983. These sections provide that in residential sales, where the seller carries back a portion or all of the purchase price, the licensee, called the "arranger of credit," is responsible for providing a detailed **"Seller Financing Disclosure Statement."** This statement details the terms of the loans being assumed or taken "subject to", reminds the parties that a request for notice of default is available, notes whether the buyer is taking any cash out of the escrow, and in effect cautions the seller to check the buyer's credit-worthiness.

CAUTION

The Seller Financing Disclosure Statement is required where an all-inclusive deed of trust or installment land contract is used, since these instruments normally reflect an extension of credit by the seller. Since it has not been common for sellers to extend credit in connection with sales for several years, the relatively inexperienced agent can easily overlook this particular disclosure requirement.

52

3. Condominiums

Disclosures regarding condominiums or townhouses require special care. Both condominiums and townhouses (usually referred to as planned unit developments) are now treated as "common interest developments." The various statutory provisions covering the organization of legal matters in these projects is called the Davis-Stirling Common Interest Development Act.[81]

Agents can be confused about the distinction between condominiums and planned unit developments. In a condominium, the unit involves the airspace, usually to the interior unfinished walls, of the unit. Each unit owner then owns an undivided interest as a tenant-in-common in the underlying land and the structures supporting the airspace. These areas, which

---

[81]Calif. Civil Code §1350 *et seq.* adopted in 1985. For an excellent summary of the law see Spraul, *Common Interest Community Associations and Their Management Structure* (Dec. 1993) California Real Property Journal, available from the Journal at 23285 Eichler Street, Unit A, Hayward, CA 94545.

include doors, studding, roof, walls, and foundations, are referred to as the common area. A condominium project comes into being at the time the first unit is conveyed. Prior to that time, even if the developer has obtained all the governmental approvals and recorded all the documents necessary to subdivide and sell individual condominiums, the property still is not a condominium subject to the condominium laws.

Planned unit developments, on the other hand, consist of sub-standard lots. The lot owner owns the lot and the structure on it in fee simple. An association owns the common areas which are usually driveways, walkways, landscaping, swimming pools, and other recreational facilities. This common area normally is deeded to the association at the time of the first sale. Practically speaking, there is little difference between a condominium and a planned unit since they both are run by associations, and the regulations and obligations are very similar. For example, even though a lot owner in a planned unit development owns the exterior of his unit, he is nevertheless prohibited by the covenants, conditions, and restrictions from altering or changing the outside of the unit without the permission of the homeowners' association.

CAUTION ▶

53

In transactions involving either a condominium or a planned unit development lot, the transfer disclosure statement must be completed by the seller and the agents as with any other residential sale. The agents, however, do not have to make any inspection of the common area and need only make a visual inspection of the unit or lot involved. This limitation is helpful because often the agent cannot be aware of structural problems in the common area.

Civil Code section 1368 also provides that, prior to close of escrow, any purchaser of a condominium or planned development must be provided with all the governing documents of the common interest development as well as the homeowner association's latest financial statement, and a statement regarding fees and unpaid assessments. Management documents that must be furnished are normally the articles of incorporation or articles of association,[82] the bylaws, and the declaration (which used to

---

[82] "Articles of Incorporation" are filed with the Secretary of State for a non-profit corporation. "Articles of Association" are for an unincorporated association and are not filed with any governmental agency. Both are used in common interest developments, although filing articles of incorporation is generally felt to be the preferable practice.

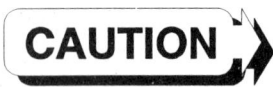

be referred to as the covenants, conditions and restrictions).[83]

Most homeowners' associations, or the property managers acting on behalf of the board of directors, prepare a standard form regarding the amount of homeowners dues; delinquencies; and special assessments or fees approved by the board of directors but not yet due or payable. This statement is very important. Litigation often results because a statement obtained from the management of the homeowners association does not accurately reflect problems that have occurred and assessments that might be contemplated but have not yet been imposed. If the agent has even the slightest question as to a statement's accuracy, further inquiry is required.[84]

Recent cases also indicate that every purchaser of a condominium or a townhouse should also be cautioned about obtaining individual liability insurance, even though the homeowners association may have coverage. In the case of *Ruoff v. Harbor Creek Community Assn.*,[85] the court held that individual unit owners who also hold an undivided interest in the common area are liable for damages caused by defects in the common area. In that case the plaintiff suffered severe injuries requiring lifetime care. The homeowners association insurance policy limit of $1,000,000 was inadequate, and the court held that individual unit owners could therefore be held liable for the excess.

This liability problem often is not present in planned unit developments where the common area is usually (though not always) owned by the association. In condominiums, however, the unit owner always holds an undivided interest in the common area with the other unit owners. Until legislation is passed providing immunity to the individual unit owners, the Standard of Care may well require agents to advise the prospective purchaser of this possible exposure.

An example of the problems involved in making adequate disclosures in common interest subdivision cases is demonstrated in a case involving a Northern California project located on a lagoon created by the original developers of the project. The

54

CAUTION

---

[83]Under §1351(h) of the Davis-Stirling Act, the covenants, conditions and restrictions are simply now referred to as "the declaration."

[84]The financial information must be provided by the association within ten days after the seller/owner requests it or the association is liable for actual damages plus a civil penalty of up to $500 and attorney's fees. See Calif. Civil Code §1368.

[85](1993) 10 Cal.App.4th 1624; 13 Cal.Rptr.2d 755.

lagoon was intended to act as a boat dock for the condominium owners that had units located on it and to provide deep water access to the San Francisco Bay. Since the project was a planned unit development project with very little common area to be maintained other than the lagoon, the monthly assessment was modest — about $20. The lagoon had to be dredged from time to time because it silted up and as such would provide deep water access only during relatively high tide periods. In the past homeowners got together and individually contributed $3,000 each for dredging when necessary, which was about every five years. However, in recent years certain water actions increased the silting process considerably. It became apparent that substantial dredging would soon be necessary. The homeowners' association had accumulated insufficient reserves to pay for the dredging. While the problem was discussed in the monthly newsletter, it was not specifically addressed in the financial statements produced by the homeowners association.

With regard to delinquent assessments and other financial matters, the form failed to mention a financial problem regarding dredging. Consequently several purchasers were not informed that without dredging they could not get their boats from the lagoon to the San Francisco Bay. One suit was brought against the homeowners' association to establish they had a duty under the declaration to maintain the lagoon. The court found that such a duty did exist and ordered the homeowners association to prepare a plan. The homeowners' association appealed the decision which is still pending.

55

Three other homeowners brought individual suits seeking damages from the sellers and the agents of both buyers and sellers for not revealing the lagoon's siltation problem and the homeowners association's failure to secure enough reserve funds to pay for dredging on a regular basis. In all three cases evidence showed that when supplying information about existing or contemplated special assessments in each transaction, the homeowners' association indicated that no special assessments were contemplated and mentioned nothing about a serious lagoon problem. In one case, the listing agent indicated in the disclosure statement that the lagoon required dredging every five years or so. The purchasers all indicated they thought the assessments were sufficient to take care of any lagoon maintenance, even though they knew the assessments were very modest. The agents claimed they did not have a duty to investigate beyond what the sellers and homeowners' association told them about the condition of the lagoon or the assessments necessary to maintain it.

Shortly before trial, all three cases settled for amounts ranging from $56,750 to $75,000. A substantial portion of the settlements came from the brokers involved, even though there was substantial conflict among experts as to whether the agents had acted within the Standard of Care. The simple reality of the situation is where there is a reasonable possibility of a finding of liability by a jury, and the cost of defending the case is between $20,000 to $30,000, the prudent economic course of action is to try to settle for a "reasonable" amount.

However, the question remains whether the agents, who all testified they saw boats riding high in the water and knew absolutely nothing about a dredging problem, had a duty to press the homeowners' association about any problems in maintaining the lagoon and whether sufficient financial reserves were available for that purpose. An examination of financial statements by the agent would clearly have revealed little or no reserves for dredging. The agents uniformly said they did not routinely study financial statements, and their backgrounds would not give them sufficient expertise to determine the sufficiency of the reserves even if they did examine the statements.

RECOMMEND

While it seems clear the agents did not have to go from door to door and ask other owners about problems, the question remains whether the agent has a duty to make some sort of an analysis of the financial statements received to see whether or not there are adequate reserves. Whether this duty is imposed upon the agents is not clear and there are no cases addressing the question. Thus, a prudent agent indicates on the disclosure statement or separately that the purchaser should make an independent investigation of association financial statements to ascertain if ample reserves are held for replacements and maintenance of the common areas.

RECOMMEND

Professional Publishing has developed a disclosure supplement especially for condominiums.[86] While it addresses most of the concerns mentioned, it does not make reference to the insurance question raised by the *Ruoff* case. Pending revision of the form, it is recommended that the following note be made on the form:

Since Buyers own the common areas as tenants in common, they should obtain personal liability insurance

---

[86]Professional Publishing, 122 Paul Drive, San Rafael, CA 94903 (Telephone 800-288-2006), Form Nos. 110.35 and 110.36.

56

in the event that the insurance carried by the homeowners' association is not adequate.

4. Special Disclosures

Although not often the subject of litigation, a number of special disclosures must be made if a residence is located in certain areas. In the name of consumer protection, Congress and the State Legislature have seen fit to add a number of requirements to already burdened sellers. The agent has a duty to be familiar with these special disclosures and inquire whether they are applicable.

▶ *Mello-Roos Disclosure.* In 1982 the Mello-Roos Community Facilities Act authorized formation of community facilities districts which could levy special taxes to build community facilities. By amendment effective July 1, 1993, the seller of residential property subject to the lien of a Mello-Roos district must make a good faith effort to obtain from the district a disclosure notice concerning the special tax and give the notice to a prospective purchaser.

▶ *Smoke Detector Compliance.* The seller must provide the buyer with a written statement representing the property is in compliance with California law regarding smoke detectors. In new home construction, the smoke detector must be wired, with a battery backup. In existing dwellings, only a battery operated detector is required.

▶ *Lead-based Paint Hazards.* If the residence was built prior to 1978 and a federally related mortgage is involved, the prospective buyer must receive and sign a receipt for a prescribed notice concerning lead-based paint hazards.

▶ *Fire Risk.* If property is known by the seller to be located in areas posing substantial fire risks (classified as state responsibility areas), this must be disclosed to the buyer. The seller must also disclose that the state is not obligated to provide fire protection services for any building or structure unless such protection is required by a cooperative agreement with a county, city, or district.

▶ *Earthquake Zones.* With some exceptions, a seller of real property situated in a special studies zone (as shown on maps prepared by the State Division of Mines and Geology) must disclose to the buyer that the property is or may be

57

situated in the zone, as designated under the Alquist-Priolo Special Studies Zones Act.

RECOMMEND

58

► *Toxic Contamination.* A number of state and federal laws relate to environmental hazards. The field has become so complex that major law firms have departments specializing in nothing else. Most commercial transactions now require a Phase I toxic examination, if for no other reason than a lender will not fund a loan without it. If this report indicates possible contamination, then a Phase II investigation (which involves drilling test holes in the soil) is required. Even if there is no loan involved, or there is seller carry-back financing, toxic tests should be conducted or written waivers obtained in all commercial building transactions.

To a lesser degree the problem can extend to residential property. Oil tanks for home heating often were buried in the ground and may pose a toxic threat. The Transfer Disclosure Statement now requires sellers to disclose whether they know of the presence of hazardous substances. If there are any questions at all, a prospective buyer should be asked to sign a receipt for a hazard disclosure addendum and should be provided with the booklet on the subject prepared by the Office of Environmental Health Hazard Assessment.

► *Flood Zones.* A seller of real property located in a special flood hazard area must disclose the fact to a buyer, and mention that federal law requires flood insurance as a condition of obtaining financing on most residences located in a special flood hazard area. However, agents must be careful to avoid giving insurance counseling since this exposes the agent to future litigation if the insurance proves to be inadequate. Make certain the buyer contacts an insurance broker before the escrow closes.

► *Title Insurance.* If for some reason the buyer does not intend to get title insurance, Civil Code section 1057.6 requires the buyer to acknowledge a special notice in the escrow reading:

> "IMPORTANT: IN A PURCHASE OR EXCHANGE OF REAL PROPERTY, IT MAY BE ADVISABLE TO OBTAIN TITLE INSURANCE IN CONNECTION WITH THE CLOSE OF ESCROW SINCE THERE MAY BE PRIOR RECORDED LIENS AND ENCUMBRANCES WHICH AFFECT YOUR INTEREST IN THE PROPERTY BEING ACQUIRED. A NEW POLICY OF TITLE INSURANCE SHOULD BE OBTAINED IN ORDER TO ENSURE YOUR INTEREST IN THE PROPERTY THAT YOU ARE ACQUIRING."

So much for crediting the buyer or the buyer's agent with minimum intelligence. If the legislature believes agents cannot handle this fairly simple task, it is puzzling that courts bestow them with all sorts of skills when they are sued.

D. Recurring Disclosure Problems

Claims by buyers that they have been deceived because sellers failed to disclose problems with the property constitute the primary basis of all litigation concerning residential real property sales. The failure to disclose repeatedly involves the same types of situations. If an agent is alert to these particular problems, which number less than a dozen, he or she has reduced the probability of being involved in litigation by at least ninety percent. A big step towards effective personal risk management involves taking the time to examine these areas in which litigation most often occurs.

How to Avoid Lawsuits

☒ 90 % of all litigation involves failure to disclose
☒ 90% of all failure to disclose cases involve one or more of the following problems:

☑ Lack of Building Permit
☑ Defective Septic Tank
☑ Leaking Roof - Drainage
☑ Boundary Lines
☑ Condominium Reserves
☑ Deck Supports & Railings
☑ Sloping Floors - Distortions
☑ Lack of Tempered Glass
☑ Pet Odors

59

1. Lack of Building Permit & Illegal Second Unit

One of the joys, and sometimes frustration, of owning a home is being able to make repairs, additions and improvements to the property. Homeowners often proceed without the benefit of a building permit, which is required for almost all improvements. Even a roof replacement requires a building permit in some jurisdictions. Certainly rewiring, changing walls, adding rooms and almost any extensive remodeling, even though not necessarily of a structural nature, calls for a building permit.

Some homeowners do not honestly realize a permit is required for what they undertake. However, for the most part the homeowner is simply trying to avoid paying the fee imposed for obtaining the permit. Sometimes these fees can be substantial and constitute a primary source of income for the local governmental authority. Whatever the motivation, a number of

60

RECOMMEND

homeowners simply avoid or refuse to apply for or obtain a permit for additions.

Many homeowners also assume if they hire a contractor to do any alterations for them, the contractor will obtain the building permit. However, even licensed contractors often avoid obtaining building permits, apparently for the same reason — to avoid paying the permit fee. The homeowner should always ask the contractor for a copy of the permit or make certain the permit is posted at the site being repaired or remodeled.

Failure to obtain a building permit often triggers two claims by buyers: (1) that a permit was not obtained and (2) that the modifications were not done in compliance with building codes. Normally, if a licensed contractor is used, modifications are done in compliance with building codes. If a non-licensed contractor is used, or the homeowner does the modifications, building codes frequently are not followed. These two items are covered in questions C4 and C5 of the Transfer Disclosure Statement. When the seller answers either of these questions "no," indicating that no additions or modifications were made without permits or out of compliance with building codes, the question arises as to what effort is required on the part of the real estate agent to verify the accuracy of that answer.

While experts differ on the degree of verification required, they agree that under certain circumstances some verification is necessary to comply with the ordinary Standard of Care. If remodeling or additions to the property are evident, the agent is required to make specific inquiry of the seller whether a building permit was obtained and, if so, **should ask to see a copy of it**. Examining the permit will indicate whether or not the building inspector signed off the section labeled "final inspection." Oddly enough, sometimes homeowners obtain building permits and never bother to have the alteration or modification inspected or signed off with a final inspection.

If the seller has no evidence of obtaining a building permit and final inspection, it is incumbent on the agent to inquire of the local building department whether or not a permit was obtained and finalized. Normally this can be done by telephone. However, in some jurisdictions the building department requires that you come in before producing the file for you to examine.

Sometimes agents testify in their deposition they did go to the building department to determine the property's building permit history only to find the file so confusing they did not understand what they examined. The building department is there to serve us. Do not hesitate to ask for help. Make a memorandum for your file of the date and time of the visit to the building department concerning this property, or the date and time of the telephone inquiry, and the specific results.

Many agents mistakenly assume that in those jurisdictions requiring residential building reports in connection with any sale or transfer of residential real property, it is not necessary to make any inquiry about building permits since the building inspector will note this on his inspection report. Absolutely not true! Rarely does the inspector check records to see whether any permits have been pulled for an addition, or whether they have been signed off. The inspector sometimes make notes whether the unit is legal, or legal but non-conforming, or any other zoning status. Often even this is not done. The inspection's primary purpose is for safety, i.e., to see whether smoke detectors are installed and other building and safety requirements met. For example, the inspector may require hand rail installation or tempered glass replacement if it poses a danger. Sometimes no one comes out to see the property at all when a residential inspection report is requested, leading one to believe the only reason for requiring the report is for additional municipal income.

CAUTION

61

The law is also very clear that if the person making the inspection fails to note some defect in the property, absolutely no liability falls on the inspector, the city, or the county.

2. Lack of Tempered Glass

In the 1950s and 1960s a great many Eichler homes were built in the San Francisco Bay area, as well as in some areas of Southern California. These homes were innovative in using floor to ceiling glass in many areas, giving an open feeling and creating an environment where the inside and outside of the residence blended together. Unfortunately, when most of the Eichler homes were constructed, the Uniform Building Code did not require tempered glass in construction. Since then the Uniform Building Code has been amended to require that all glass elements of a house located within 18 inches of the floor be safety glass or tempered glass. With untempered glass, wooden bars or other protective devices must be installed.

In several cases the owners of Eichler homes have walked through, been thrown through, or fallen through the glass window-walls, particularly those immediately adjacent to sliding glass doors. Injuries sustained can be very serious. In litigated cases, including one where an attorney-husband threw his wife through the window in a drunken dispute, one cannot help but generate sympathy for the victim.

Seeking compensation for these injuries, the victim files suit against the seller and the agents for not disclosing the lack of safety or tempered glass panels and doors. The basis for these claims usually rests in a decision called the *Becker* case,[87] decided some years ago, where the court held an apartment house owner liable to a tenant when the tenant injured himself falling through an untempered shower glass door. While the *Becker* case hardly seems to support liability on the part of sellers of residential real property, much less the agents involved in the sale, the Eichler glass cases are resulting in settlements, albeit relatively modest, to injured purchasers. In one case an expert witness for the plaintiff purchaser testified that it was common knowledge that Eichler homes were built of easily broken glass and that agents should know what is common knowledge in the locations where they sell homes.

This expert is suggesting that agents have a duty to examine glass panels on floor to ceiling windows and sliding doors to see if they bear an emblem identifying them as safety glass. This emblem is sometimes etched into the glass or on a transparent seal in the lower or sometimes upper corner. While this might seem an unusual requirement, the "red flags inspection checklist" published by Professional Publishing (Form 109RF) has a section for the agents to answer whether they observed safety glass emblems on the sliding doors.

RECOMMEND

This author believes that failure to look for the decal on the glass does not constitute conduct below the Standard of Care. Nevertheless, to avoid exposure it is recommended, at least with Eichler homes, that agents inquire whether untempered glass has been replaced with safety glass. If not, this should be noted on the disclosure form.

62

---

[87]*Becker v. IRM Corporation* (1985) 38 Cal.3d 454; 213 Cal.Rptr. 213.

3. Pet Odors

One might reasonably assume that if a residence suffered undesirable pet odors, prospective purchasers will ascertain the odors as readily as the agents involved. After all, Civil Code section 2079.5 specifically provides that none of the inspections required of agents "relieves a buyer or prospective buyer of the duty to exercise reasonable care to protect himself or herself, including those facts which are known to or within the diligent intention and observation of the buyer or prospective buyer." The smell of cat or dog urine certainly seems to fall within the boundaries of this provision.

Unfortunately, pet odor is more serious and elusive than one might suspect. In one trial concerning failure to disclose cat urine odors, an expert on decontamination of pet odors testified at length concerning the problem. According to him, the bacteria in the floor, walls, joists, and even the 2x4s supporting the ceiling can rest dormant for long periods of time. Then, a particularly humid day, or humidity from a shower, can trigger and activate dormant bacteria producing awful odors and even making wallboard soggy.

In one particular case, the owner of a condominium was absent for several weeks, leaving two cats who were attended daily by a neighbor. The patio sliding door had been left open and litter boxes placed on the porch. However, the cats were apparently unhappy at their mistress' absence and proceeded to vent their anger by "marking" various places throughout the condominium.

When the owner decided to sell the unit, she replaced the carpeting and had the floors thoroughly cleaned and sealed. Wall vents, rusty from urine, were replaced, as were electrical outlets inoperable because of cat urine. The owner then could detect no odor.

The next owner kept the unit for a short period of time. Although she noticed some odor in the bathroom area, she simply sprayed a "pet odor eliminator" on the wall and considered the problem solved. Several people, including a local judge, who visited the unit for meetings, to play bridge, and for other activities, testified that they noticed no unusual odor.

Then a minister and his wife purchased and moved into the unit. After two weeks they began to smell odors they could not identify. They had their house plants replaced, believing the fertilizer in the soil was causing the odor. Finally, an expert advised them of pet urine odors in the wallboard and supporting wood framing. He reached this conclusion using a "urinometer,"

63

a device supposedly able to measure the amount and content of urine which had been sprayed on walls. This same expert testified at trial that in order to rid the unit of the offending odors, the walls and floors would have to be completely removed The supporting framing would have to be sanded and chemically treated, and the wallboard and floors replaced, together with all appliances. The cost of this decontamination was $175,000, which seemed excessively high compared to the unit sale price of $280,000.

The plaintiffs also obtained a copy of a prior building inspection report noting a faint odor of cat urine, which the inspector understood would be removed by replacing the carpeting and sealing the floors, which had been done. The plaintiffs alleged the agents, being aware of this possible contamination, should have warned the purchasers that an "extra special" inspection by a pet decontamination expert was necessary before escrow closed. Another expert witness was prepared to testify, but never did, that the agents acted below the Standard of Care in not fully alerting the purchasers of the possibility of future pet odor.

The jury found for the purchasers and against the seller in the sum of $40,000. They found in favor of the agents.

If pets live in the unit being sold, without question agents should inquire whether pet odors have ever been a problem. The agent section of the disclosure statement should note that pets have been in the premises and the purchasers should satisfy themselves regarding any objectionable pet odors.

64

CAUTION

4. Cracks or Visually Distorted Structures

When you look at a garage door or door frames on a house they sometimes appear to be out of plumb. This can indicate a serious condition caused by foundation or soil movement leading the structure to shift and move. Sometimes this condition shows up as cracks at the corners of windows or doors.

Sellers often employ ingenious devices to conceal this shifting of the residence. In one case the framing on the garage doors was tapered. The frame at the bottom of the door was three inches wide. By the time it got to the top of the door it was only three quarters of an inch wide. With the door shut, this gave the appearance of a perfectly rectangular structure. Not until you

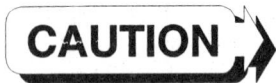

came close could you see that the framing had been tapered to allow for the shift and conceal the structural deficiency.

After this particular house was purchased, the buyer hired a civil engineer who advised that the foundation had shifted and extensive work would be required to jack up the house and re-pour the foundation. The buyer sued the seller, both agents, and the contractor who inspected the house for the buyer on the ground that they had been negligent in not discovering this condition. The seller, unfortunately, was insolvent, with little or nothing to contribute to any settlement. The agents claimed that, since the buyer had hired a licensed contractor to inspect the residence, they were not liable under the provisions of Civil Code sections 2079 and 1102, which provide that agents are not responsible for inspecting areas concerning which professional inspection reports are obtained.

The purchaser nevertheless prevailed in his cause of action, particularly against his own agent, on the ground that the agent gave him the name of only one contractor to make the inspection, and therefore was responsible for referring someone who performed negligently. The case settled with the seller and his agent making a nominal contribution, and the buyer's agent and the contractor picking up most of the cost of repairing the defect. The buyer himself absorbed about one-half of the cost of repair on the basis of arguments put forward that this shifting condition should have been apparent to him and any layman.

65

The case demonstrates why agents must be careful when recommending professionals to inspect or otherwise deal with transactions. Always give the names of at least three firms or persons, and make certain the list contains an exculpatory clause that the agent is in no way responsible for the work performed by them. The following language can be used:

CAUTION

> **The names of inspectors and other professionals listed above are given as a matter of accommodation only. The agents and broker assume no responsibility for any act or omission on the part of the inspector or professional selected.**

Even though professionals inspect the property, as a practical matter defects which can be observed visually by the agent should be disclosed in the TDS. Do not totally rely on the professional inspection.

5. Deck Supports and Railings

RECOMMEND

66

A surprisingly large number of failure-to-disclose cases involve decks without adequate supports or railings. The cost of correcting this is usually nominal compared to the cost of initiating litigation. This can lead to the conclusion that the buyer is more interested in putting on a new deck than with the inadequacies of the old deck. In fact, in many of the claims the purchaser advises the seller of the claimed deficiencies, announcing that corrective work will be undertaken immediately. The buyer then replaces the deck and railing and tries to lay the entire burden on the seller.

In the event of such a claim after escrow closes, and if the seller's agent becomes involved on behalf of the seller in handling the buyer's claim, the agent should advise the seller to contact counsel immediately and make certain a qualified person inspects the deck and railing before it is removed and restored. Take photographs of the deck in its original condition. Such documentary and expert testimony often convinces a jury that the old deck's deficiencies were relatively minor and the buyer was simply taking advantage of the situation.

The Uniform Building Code requires that all decks 30 inches or more above ground level include railings. These railings must be a minimum of 42 inches high (or in some cases 36). The openings between the uprights can be no more than six inches. The purpose of these restrictions is to prevent small children from slipping through the railing. The supports for the decks should also be inspected if visible, particularly on sloped properties, to verify the beams are adequately supported on concrete pads or piers. In some cases the slippage occurring is obvious and should be noted by the agent. The railings on the decks should be secure, not wobbly or suggesting they might give way if leaned against. Be particularly cautious when sellers say you must not go out onto the deck to look at it or the railings because their vicious dog is there. The deck should be inspected, dog or no dog! It should also be determined whether the floor of the deck is adequately installed. Numerous complaints arise where the decking material is placed very close together, not allowing for drainage. This can quickly create dry rot.

Agents should also look for any **noticeable problems** with the flashing between the deck and the structure. Sometimes decks sag towards the house, breaking the flashing connection and allowing water from the deck to penetrate inside the house. While agents are only responsible for visual inspections, if the slope of the deck is towards the house rather than away from it, further inquiry should be made.

6. Drainage Problems

One question posed on the Transfer Disclosure Statement, and often referred to again on supplemental disclosure statements, is whether the seller knows of any "flooding, drainage or grading problems." During the long drought in California, what was once a problem seemed to disappear. When the rains did come, water intrusion and standing water problems reappeared to the annoyance of unsuspecting buyers. Relying on the delayed discovery rule, which in effect suspends (or, in legalese, "tolls") the statute of limitations, buyers began filing lawsuits concerning sales which closed years earlier.

An agent is not expected to be omniscient when making the required visual inspection. If a transaction is taking place in the summer, or there has been no precipitation for a period of time, there may be little evidence of drainage problems. In one case, however, the agent noticed a substantial amount of standing water at the property's front entrance area. Round concrete steps had been laid in the water to act as stepping stones and oriental-type landscaping recently installed. When the agent asked what caused the standing water, the seller replied that they had intentionally created a Japanese water garden for aesthetic purposes. The agent repeated this representation to the buyer. After escrow closed it was learned that the so-called "garden" was merely a camouflage for a serious drainage problem costing several thousand dollars to rectify.

67

Did the agent act below the Standard of Care in not further investigating the problem? The case was settled shortly before going to trial with contributions from the broker (who had both sides of the transaction) and the seller. Consequently neither the court or jury passed upon the liability question. However, the settlement was obviously motivated by the belief that a jury could well find the agents were too easily duped and should have warned the buyer to seek professional inspection of the drainage situation.

Drainage problems are often the subject of home repairs and weekend "fixes." Most homeowners are all too familiar with digging trenches and installing drain tiles, and otherwise dealing with standing or intruding water. This type of improvement generally does not require a permit and often solves the problem — at least for a while. However, unless installed by professionals, drain systems can eventually become unserviceable and require cleaning or repair.

When reviewing the Transfer Disclosure Statement with a seller, it is prudent to ask if there have **ever been any drainage or flooding problems**. If there have been problems which were

RECOMMEND

"fixed", the date, nature of the repair, and the person or company performing it should be included in the statement. Then the buyers, if they so choose, can investigate further. They cannot, however, accuse the sellers of concealing a defective repair job.

Shortly after one closing, a buyer noticed a substantial amount of dirt sloughing down the back yard hill into the swimming pool. Investigating, he discovered the name and whereabouts of the pool company that had serviced the pool under the prior ownership. The company told the buyer that the previous owner also experienced soil sloughing into the pool after heavy rains, and tried to fix the problem, with little success. The resulting siltation damaged the pool filter and necessitated frequent cleanups.

When confronted with this evidence, the seller acknowledged there had been problems after the 1982 and 1986 storms, but insisted that, with the help of his neighbors, he had installed drains and solved the problem. He had experienced no difficulty since the heavy rains of 1986. Moreover, he testified that when he was filling out the Transfer Disclosure Statement with his agent, he told her about the repairs. When she asked him whether this had "fixed" the problem, he replied in the affirmative, and she told him that then it did not have to be mentioned since there was not a current problem. The agent could not recall any such exchange of information or advice but did not deny that it might have taken place.

68

The cost of installing a new, somewhat extravagant, drainage system was estimated at $40,000. The lawsuit was settled by a contribution from the seller of $16,500 and $6,000 from his agent. The case demonstrates the need to avoid misunderstandings and charges of concealment by **disclosing all past problems of a material nature, even though the seller may be convinced that the problem no longer exists**. This recommendation applies to all components of the property, not just drainage conditions.

RECOMMEND

There are limits to what an agent is expected to do regarding drainage conditions. In connection with a sale of a house flooded in the 1986 storms, the agent carefully pointed out to buyers that the property was in a flood zone and they would need to secure flood insurance before they could obtain a loan. The sale closed, and within a year flooding occurred. The buyers received a check for damage to the real property, but sued on the ground that they lost considerable personal property not covered by the insurance. The agent was at fault, according to the buyers, for not fully advising them of the extent of the insurance needed and the severity of the flooding. In addition, the fact that their native language was Spanish allegedly hindered them in understanding the transaction.

The court made short shrift of the plaintiffs' claims, finding the agent fully performed his function in warning the buyers of flood dangers. Other than advising the purchasers that the house was in a flood zone and they would have to get flood insurance, the agent had no duty to advise regarding the extent or nature of the necessary insurance. That the agent used fluent Spanish in conducting all the negotiations did not help the plaintiffs' claim about misunderstanding the proceedings.

7. Leaking Roofs

Hell hath no fury greater than a buyer with a leaking roof! Water intrusion is like a burglary. It causes severe emotional trauma, and is the basis of substantial litigation. Some pre-printed forms attempt to mitigate the problem. The Coldwell Banker version contains a warranty that "roofs shall be free of leaks." The CAR form gives the seller the option of initialling an "as is" provision or warranting that the "Roof shall be free of KNOWN leaks." The Professional Publishing form leaves the issue to the Real Estate Transfer Disclosure Supplement which asks: "Has roof ever leaked since you owned?" The Fox & Carskadon Supplemental Form likewise asks: "Have you experienced any leaks on the ceiling, around windows or fireplace?"

69

The difficulty with making a "no leaks" warranty is that the first rain may arrive long after the close of escrow. The defective condition may have originated after the close. A warranty against "known leaks" is not a warranty at all. It is merely a disclosure statement that the seller is not aware of any leaks and adds nothing to that already contained in the Transfer Disclosure Statement.

RECOMMEND

Clearly, it is important to advise sellers to reveal any leaks during their ownership and explain how the problem was corrected and who did it. Most litigation in this area against agents emerges when sellers tell an agent the roof leaked once but was "replaced," "repaired," "patched," or whatever. The sellers then testify the agent said "we did not have to reveal the leak if it was no longer a problem." From a technical point of view, this is a correct response because the statutory form of disclosure only asks whether there are significant defects or malfunctions in the roof. But if sellers disclose all leaks, including the detail of their repairs, the buyers cannot complain that any defect in the roof was concealed.

There is no evidence that revealing the history of roof leakage or any other water intrusion has negative impact on a sale. To the contrary, the buyers appear more comfortable knowing that both the good and bad features of the property have been fully disclosed.

8. Sloping Floors

70

The failure of the seller's agent to recognize problems revealed by sloping floors led to the seminal case of *Easton v. Strassburger.* One agent testified that he observed uneven floors in a guest house on the property. The other agent testified that uneven floors were "red flags," indicating potential soils problems. The court held that the existence of a sloping floor, together with knowledge that the house was built on fill, required that a soils report be prepared, regardless of whether the agents knew of any slides or soils problems on the property.[88]

Some writers suggest that a smooth ball, such as a racquetball, be placed on the floor to "see if it rolls."[89] This seems a bit much. Not only might your client think your conduct a little strange, but ball-rolling does not seem to fit within the requirement of a *visual* inspection.

Spongy floors, exterior steps askew, cracked fireplaces, uneven spaces between doors and windows and their frames, "pop outs" on slopes in the yard, and the presence of drainage gullies can all indicate soil instability. Any such conditions should be noted in the agent's section of the Transfer Disclosure Statement. In addition, the agent should strongly recommend conducting a soils inspection with a competent professional. If the client declines because of cost or any other reason, document

RECOMMEND

---

[88] *Easton v. Strassburger* (1984) 152 Cal.App.3d 90,104; 199 Cal.Rptr. 383, 391.

[89] Prendergast, *Red Flags Property Inspection Guide* (Professional Publishing - 1987), p. 2/25.

the fact, preferably by putting the recommendation in writing, acknowledged by the client's signature .

Many cases involve prior landslides on adjoining property. If the agent is aware of such past difficulty, or can see that slides have occurred (such as repaired "pop-outs" or failing retaining walls), the agent has a duty to note the condition, even if it is not on the property directly involved in the sale.

9. Boundary Lines

Buyers obtaining less property than they think they bargained for feel seriously cheated, even if the missing acreage has little or no impact on the property's value or desirability. Surveying is not part of the discipline of real estate agents or brokers, and they are not ordinarily required to verify the boundary lines of a parcel or determine its precise size.

Normally information used in the multiple listing or on flyers is obtained from sellers. The agent is only required to make certain the information given by sellers appears to conform with information in the preliminary title report, the assessor's map, and an ordinary visual inspection of the property. If the maps show a straight property line but the property is enclosed by zigzag fences, ask about the disparity.

71

Exposure arises when the agent makes a positive representation to the buyer regarding the location of the property line and what is included within the sale. This often happens inadvertently. In one case, an agent, holding an open house, nodded in agreement when a prospective purchaser mentioned how pleasant a gazebo looked. It turned out that the gazebo straddled the property line. The buyer, after learning of the discrepancy, promptly sued both seller and agent for misrepresenting the boundary lines. Although an appraiser testified that the gazebo had a value of $5,000, the defendants, fearing an award of punitive damages, settled the case for $65,000 midway through a jury trial.

CAUTION

In another case a buyer discovered, after signing the contract but prior to close of escrow, that the acreage was ten percent less than represented by the seller. The buyer first attempted to close with a reduction in the purchase price. The sellers told him to get lost and sold to a third party. The original buyer then acquired the property from the third party at a price increase of

$40,000 and sued the seller and the seller's agent for the $40,000 plus additional consequential damages, including the cost of a private school for the buyer's eight year old son during the period they could not occupy the house.

The case was treated as a joke by the defendants, but the humor evaporated when the trial court issued its decision. It held that the seller negligently misrepresented the boundary lines and that the seller's agent should have noticed the discrepancy between the fence lines and the boundary lines as shown on a map appended to an early title report. However, since the buyer became aware of the discrepancy before escrow closed, he was entitled only to damages of $1400 for costs incurred prior to his discovery. The court further found no "prevailing party" and declined to award attorney fees, by that time reaching tens of thousands of dollars for each party. Whew! A close call for the seller's agent.

Often boundary-line litigation becomes complicated because it involves quiet title actions, prescriptive easements, adverse possession, agreed-upon boundaries, and other complex issues. The parties are not usually amenable to settlement. In one recent case an owner of a duplex, learning that his neighbor's improvements encroached on his property, destroyed a fence and jack-hammered the patio in the middle of the night while the neighbor was out of town. It took weeks of patient negotiation to bring the parties to a settlement posture.

At one time title insurance companies offered ALTA Owner's Policies to buyers, similar to ALTA Lender's Policies. These protected against many off-record defects such as liens, encumbrances, easements and encroachments. Except for the expense of a survey, if required, the cost was about the same as a Standard CLTA policy. Recently, however, changes have been made so that a Residential ALTA Owner's Policy excepts (1) any easement not shown by the public record, and (2) any facts about the land which a correct survey would describe and which is not shown by the public record. Unless you have a good understanding of the difference between the policies, recommend that the buyer obtain an explanation from the title officer involved in the transaction.

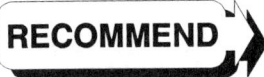

RECOMMEND ▶

Most pre-printed forms now contain a disclaimer regarding representations concerning boundary lines and the size of the parcel. If the form you use does not contain such a disclaimer, or you are uncomfortable with its adequacy, do not hesitate to add to the Transfer Disclosure Statement (append another sheet if necessary) the following:

72

The Broker has not been informed by Sellers of the precise boundaries of the property and neither Sellers nor Broker makes any representations regarding boundary locations or the size of the parcel except as may be shown on the preliminary title report. It is recommended that if purchaser has any questions in this regard, the purchaser should obtain a survey and also acquire an ALTA Owners Title Insurance Policy which can give greater coverage than the CLTA Standard Coverage Policy. Your title company can explain the extended coverage and what additional cost, if any, is involved.

10. And Others

There are those purchasers whose complaints about failure to disclose are simply unreasonable and cannot be avoided no matter how much care is taken. For example, in one townhouse complex several units were located on a dead-end street. The garbage truck had to back up to the units to pick up weekly refuse. When the truck did this, it made the beep - beep - beep sound required whenever commercial equipment is operated in reverse. The buyer threatened to sue because he was not warned this noise was going to occur every Saturday morning. After putting all parties to considerable grief, he abandoned the threat of suit.

In another case an agent purchased, for her own account and for her son, a small business her broker had listed for sale. After a year of operation, the business failed. The agent sued her broker for failure to disclose adequate income and expense statements and for negligence in letting her represent herself as buyer because she was incompetent. The judge directed a verdict in favor of the defendant broker, shaking his head in disbelief!

A buyer sought to recover damages from a seller where the septic system was found to be inadequate for the buyer's needs. Those needs included a kennel with thirty dogs. When the county notified the buyer that his operation required something special in the way of a disposal system, the buyer's first thought was to sue the seller for fraud. The buyer was ultimately persuaded to abandon the suit.

Zoning occasionally causes problems, even in residential sales. In one case, a psychiatrist purchased a residential home in a quiet neighborhood ideally situated for treating his patients. The building inspection report noted that the property was

73

zoned C-2, permitting a small office. However, another ordinance precluded any conversion of residential property to commercial purposes. The doctor told the agent not to make any inquiries because he did not want the neighbors to know about his intended use. He remodeled the house and conducted his practice there for several months. The county discovered his activity when he applied for a business license and ordered him to cease and desist. The doctor resold the house for a substantial profit. Nevertheless, he sued the agent for lost profits of hundreds of thousands of dollars. The court awarded damages of $100, making the doctor so furious he never bothered to collect.

In cases like these, an agent must simply accept being sued as a part of the exposure attendant to doing business with the public. Usually these meritless cases receive prompt disposal. Typically they pose little threat of monetary loss, except the cost and trauma of defense.

For the most part, an agent alert to the recurring problems that have been discussed, dramatically reduces the risk of being sued. Attention to detail and common sense can save a lot of grief.

74

Part IV
Common Drafting Problems

Although many litigants are too embarrassed to admit it, most of them fail to read or understand all of the provisions of the purchase agreement. This cultural malaise has been called "fine print" phobia.[90] It is a good idea to give the seller, when taking the listing, and any serious prospective purchaser, a copy of the contract form most frequently used in your area. Encourage your clients to read it and ask questions about any language they do not clearly understand. Be prepared to explain required provisions regarding arbitration and other complex provisions so that they thoroughly understand the agreement and any options they have when presenting an offer. Remember the law holds that a party signing a contract responsible for compliance with all of its provisions, even though the party may not have read or understood them.[91]

75

Purchase agreements should be written in clear, concise, simple words and sentences.[92] Pre-printed forms should be selected for their clarity and straight forwardness. Do not be misled because a form is produced by an association of real estate brokers or agents. These forms are often generated by large committees with varied interests to satisfy. They often try to protect the broker from liability by using needlessly complex and convoluted language.

The California Association of Realtors' purchase agreement provides the following regarding seller financing:

8. The addition, deletion, or substitution of any person or entity under this agreement, or to title prior to close of escrow, shall require Seller's written

---

[90] Dian Hymer, *Starting Out*, San Francisco Examiner, Sunday, March 7, 1993, p. F-1.

[91] *Carleton v. Tortosa* (1993) 14 Cal.App.4th 745; 17 Cal.Rptr.2d 734.

[92] For an excellent and delightful manual on techniques of understandable writing, see Goldfarb & Raymond, *Clear Understandings — A Guide to Legal Writing* (1982) Random House, New York.

consent. Seller may grant or withhold consent in Seller's sole discretion. Any additional or substituted person or entity shall, if requested by Seller, submit to Seller the same documentation as required for the original named Buyer. Seller and/or broker(s) may obtain a credit report on any such person or entity.

The same result could have been reached by simply stating: "In case of seller financing, this contract is not assignable."

The courts hold that it is a breach of an agent's fiduciary duty to use a contract containing language the buyer and seller cannot readily understand. As discussed in detail at pages 102-103, *infra*, the use of dual agency disclosure in a purchase agreement which failed to clearly inform the parties of their relationship to the agent led to a class action lawsuit. The trial court held the use of the form to be a breach of fiduciary duty. The litigation was reportedly settled for $21,000,000!

If you have difficulty in understanding the meaning of contract language, use a different form.

The "fine print phobia" also comes into play whenever any fine print is crossed out or answered "no." For example, the current Professional Publishing Form provides:

SUPPLEMENT TO STATUTORY DISCLOSURE STATEMENT. ☐ Seller shall provide the following disclosure supplement to Buyer: ☐ PPC Form 110.31/32 CAL, SUPPLEMENT TO RETDS, ☐ PPC FORM 110.35/36 CAL, CONDOMINIUM DISCLOSURE SUPPLEMENT ☐ Other:_____

Many brokers feel that some of the matters covered in the supplemental disclosure statement may be objectionable, but they advise sellers to provide the form because the failure to check the box may lead some purchasers to suspect an ominous undisclosed defect. As a result, the supplemental form is almost always used.

The following discussion identifies the most common problems occurring in the contract drafting stage. Reference is made to the most frequently used residential purchase agreements in California, namely, the "Real Estate Purchase Contract and Receipt for Deposit" produced by the California Association of Realtors, the "Residential Purchase Agreement and Deposit Receipt" produced by Professional Publishing of San Rafael, and, as an example of what this author considers one of the best privately used agreements, the "Real Estate Purchase Contract" by Coldwell Banker.

76

A. The Parties to the Contract

The parties to the contract must be properly identified. The "seller" must include all of the parties on title. If not, the signing "sellers" may not be able to convey title and may be held liable by a disappointed buyer for falsely misrepresenting their authority to sell the property. While the buyer cannot get specific performance of the contract, he or she could recover damages from the persons who signed, since the act of accepting an offer or making a counteroffer carries the implied promise that the signatories can deliver the goods.[93] Of course, a careful buyer's agent will see that the preliminary report lists persons other than the signing seller as owners of the property. Immediate inquiry must then be made. If a satisfactory explanation is not given, the "Examination of Title" clause in the contract should be invoked and the seller notified of the objection. Even if the agreement is then terminated, the persons who signed the contract as purported owners may be liable for costs and expenses incurred by the buyer to the date of termination.

There may be an obligation on the agent's part to make certain that his or her client is really the owner of the property involved. The strange case of Charles Fozz[94] serves as an example. Mr. Fozz owned several acres of landlocked undeveloped land that the Marin County Open Space District had coveted for years. However, Fozz had always asked more for the land than the District could afford and negotiations never progressed very far.

One day a well-known brokerage firm received a call from Fozz advising that if a deal could be closed by the end of the year for tax purposes, he would be willing to reduce the price by $200,000. The brokers excitedly contacted the District and began negotiations. Fozz asked that the listing agreement be delivered by messenger to his San Francisco office, where it was signed and returned to the broker. The Open Space District realized it could not raise the funds in time to close on the specified date and solicited the help of a charitable land acquisition trust to purchase the property long enough to permit the District to float a bond issue.

77

---

[93]In *Baird v. Jones* (1993) 94 C.D.O.S. 113, the seller and his agent were held liable for making a counteroffer to "test the waters," knowing that without the signature of the seller's wife the counteroffer would not be binding.

[94]A fictitious name is used to protect the privacy of the party involved.

All parties cooperated, and escrow instructions were prepared by the title company following telephone directions received from Fozz and his agent. All documents, including the deed, were delivered by messenger. At the closing, Fozz was out of town, but closing papers again were delivered to him and notarized by a local notary. The escrow proceeds were delivered by messenger to Fozz's San Francisco office. The District ultimately raised the necessary funds with a bond issue and repurchased the land from the trust.

All was well until Mr. Fozz came back into town and, on discovering that his land had been sold, promptly announced he had never authorized any such transaction. He sued to set aside the deed. An investigation by local authorities and the FBI revealed that someone impersonating Fozz had set up a phony San Francisco office complete with door signs, telephone listings, and the works. The notary who supposedly acknowledged the deed did not exist in the roster of California notaries. Handwriting experts verified that the deed had been cleverly forged. The disbursement check had been negotiated through a precious coin dealer who had exchanged several hundred thousand dollars of gold coins for the check. The brokers, the District, the trust fund, and the title company had been swindled.

While one must stand in awe of this crook's cleverness, the citizens of the Open Space District were left holding bonds, the proceeds of which were used to buy property they no longer owned. The title company was liable for the forgery — but only up to the amount of the sale price. Fozz now wanted his original purchase price, which was a few hundred thousand more than the title policy.

What about the broker and the agents involved? After all, they represented that their client was Mr. Fozz. Are they liable for negligently representing that their client owned the property? The broker contended that it is not customary to ask people for their driver's license or any other identification when obtaining a listing. Moreover, it is not unusual to take listings over the telephone from out-of-state clients and handle the transaction by fax or mail.

The intriguing issue of broker liability was never solved because the parties contributed enough funds, along with the title insurance proceeds, to buy the property from the real Mr. Fozz. (Some diehards still believe that the handwriting experts made a mistake and that the elderly Mr. Fozz suffered a memory lapse.) In any event, it pays to verify that your client is really the person he or she purports to be. Government Code section 206 now requires notaries to include in their notary book the thumbprint of any person signing a deed or deed of trust affecting real estate in Los Angeles County. If successful, the law will be extended throughout the state.

Some purchase agreement forms have signature blocks for the brokers and agents of the respective parties. Why do brokers and agents sign the purchase agreement? It must be because they want to see their name in writing — there is no other good reason. There are lots of reasons not to sign the contract.

Sometimes the purchase agreement form is labeled "Residential Purchase Agreement *and Deposit Receipt.*" However, since the deposit is most often made to the title company and held in the escrow, with a separate receipt issued by the title company, this additional language in the caption of the purchase agreement is superfluous. Usually brokers hold the deposit to take advantage of any bank interest benefits they can get — the "float." This is a questionable practice. Moreover, when there is a dispute between the parties as to who is entitled to the deposit, the holder of the deposit is often named as a party. Otherwise, the court would not have jurisdiction to force the deposit holder to turn the deposit over to the proper party. Sometimes the escrow holder must "interplead" the deposit, that is, offer to turn it over to the court for ultimate disposition. All of this hassle can easily be avoided by the broker insisting the money be placed with the title company as escrow holder. If for some reason the broker decides to hold a deposit, it is simpler to issue a separate receipt than include it in the contract itself.

79

There is no good reason for the agents, for themselves or on behalf of their broker, to execute the purchase agreement. Agents are not parties to the agreement — only the seller and buyer are the proper parties. Drafting the agreement does not make brokers or their agents parties. Attorneys drafting contracts do not become parties nor do their names appear unless under a section labeled "Approved as to Form." Similarly, a broker can comply with Real Estate Regulations requiring that the contract be reviewed, dated, and initialed,[95] simply by initialing and dating the contract under the phrase "Reviewed by: ___"

Instructions in the Department of Real Estate Reference Book (1989-90 ed. at p. 637) to the effect that the agent should sign the offer on behalf of the broker **are in error and should not be followed**. It is also questionable, and certainly not nec-

CAUTION

---

[95]10 Calif. Code of Regulation §2725(a).

essary, that the broker sign the acceptance clause as urged in the DRE instructions.

As is discussed in some detail later, the Court of Appeals in *Xerueb v. Marcus & Millichap, Inc.*[96] held that agents signing an agreement are parties to the agreement for certain purposes. In particular, an agent who is caught up in a dispute between the seller and buyer over some failure to disclose could be held liable for tens of thousands of dollars in attorney fees if he or she is found to be even slightly responsible for the disclosure dispute.

The view that brokers and agents are not parties to the buy-sell agreement was confirmed in the case of *Super 7 Motel Associates v. Wang.*[97] There the court found that a broker could not take advantage of the attorney fees clause in the purchase agreement because the broker is not a party to the purchase agreement. "Although the [broker] was mentioned in the contract as the broker, he had no contractual obligations or interest in the sale of the property. He was neither obliged nor able to convey title or otherwise satisfy the seller's obligations; he was not obliged to satisfy any of the buyer's obligations; and he had no contractual duty under the purchase contract to assist either party in discharging obligations under the contract." The broker's signature found in the Acceptance part of the contract, relating to the obligation of the seller to pay a commission, does not make the broker a party to the purchase agreement. The court also noted by way of footnote that the buyer and seller "could modify the agreement without the broker's signature," further indicating he was not a "party" to the agreement.

The standard agreement should be viewed exactly as it is intended, namely **(1) a receipt for the deposit of funds by the buyer; (2) a contract between the buyer and seller setting forth the terms of the sale and purchase; and (3) the contract by which the seller agrees to pay a commission to the broker.**[98] Care should be taken to keep these three parts separate and not inadvertently make the broker a party to the buy-sell agreement. The CAR form invites the broker to initial the mediation and arbitration sections of the purchase agreement. It then provides "The initialling of this paragraph shall not result in the Broker(s) being deemed a party to the purchase and sale agreement." By initialing the agreement they probably

---

[96] (1992) 3 Cal.App.4th 1338; 5 Cal.Rptr.2d 154.

[97] (1993) 16 Cal.App.4th 541; 20 Cal.Rptr.2d 193.

[98] See 1 Miller & Starr, California Real Estate (2d ed. 1989) *Specific Real Estate Contracts* §2:32, p. 630.

have become parties and any protestation to the contrary will probably have little effect in court.

The danger of making any reference to the broker in the body of the agreement is demonstrated in the case of *Ujhazi v. Bunker*.[99] The court held that where the buyers' and their agents' "signatures appear side-by-side on the last page of the contract just above the seller's acceptance," the agents become parties to the contract and are bound by the attorney's fee clause. Although attempting to distinguish the *Super 7* case, the decision appears clearly erroneous since the agent is not a consensual party to the buy-sell portion of the contract.

Brokers and agents suffer an almost psychotic compulsion to affix their signatures to the purchase agreement — perhaps to prove they are the architects of the deal, or out of fear they will somehow be deprived of a commission unless they their signatures appear on the document. Signing the document does nothing to enhance their right to a commission and can only cause grief. Let it alone!!

B. The Attorney's Fees Clause

It has long been the rule in this country that parties must bear their own attorney's fees in most legal actions. For example, in automobile accident cases the plaintiff, if he or she recovers, must pay the attorney out of the award. California law specifically provides in Code of Civil Procedure section 1021 that unless the parties provide otherwise in writing, they must bear their own attorney fees. This led to the practice of attorneys providing in contracts that in the event of a dispute concerning the contract, the prevailing party is entitled to recover his or her reasonable attorney fees. In tort actions (which are all wrongs other than breach of contract), however, attorney fees are not recoverable. Consequently, when an agent was sued for professional negligence, failure to disclose, breach of fiduciary duty, or even fraud, it was assumed that the exposure facing the agent (and the broker who usually indemnifies the agent) was limited to actual damages incurred and did not include the plaintiff's attorney fees.

This belief was suddenly shattered by the court in *Xuereb v. Marcus & Millichap, Inc.*[100] The court held that language in the

81

---

[99](1993) 20 Cal.App.4th 1510, 25 Cal.Rptr.2d 272. (Ordered depublished by the California Supreme Court on March 17, 1994.)

[100](1992) 3 Cal.App.4th 1338; 5 Cal.Rptr.2d 154.

contract was broad enough to include attorney fees in tort actions as well as actions for breach of contract. The language in question provided: "Attorneys' Fees: If this Agreement gives rise to a lawsuit or other legal proceeding between any of the parties hereto, including Agent, the prevailing party shall be entitled to recover actual court costs and reasonable attorneys' fees in addition to any other relief to which such party may be entitled." The decision was followed in a number of subsequent cases, although these involved disputes between the buyer and seller, and attorney fees were not claimed either against or on behalf of the agent or broker.[101]

The *Xuereb* case caused considerable concern because the real estate agent loses lawsuits most of the time — with most of the effort being spent keeping the judgment to a reasonable and realistic amount. With the possibility of recovering attorney's fees motivating the plaintiff's lawyers, reasonable pre-trial settlements are much more difficult to negotiate. Prudence suggests not expanding the recovery of attorney fees to tort actions involving brokers or agents.

At the urging of counsel for many real estate brokerage firms, both CAR and Professional Publishing hastened to revise their forms, eliminating any reference to the brokers or agents in the attorney fee provision. (Coldwell Banker had long ago eliminated any such reference in its form.)

CAUTION

Eliminating any reference to the broker or agent in the purchase and sale agreement, together with the holding of *Super 7 Motel Associates v. Wang* [102] that brokers are not ordinarily parties to the agreement, should solve the problem raised by the *Xereub* case. However, **if the contract form you use refers to the agents or brokers in its attorney fee provision, be certain to strike the reference or use another form of agreement.**

As between the buyer and seller, it is now well established that the attorney fee clause entitles the prevailing party to recover attorney fees whether the action be for tort (negligence or fraud) or for breach of contract. While the court has the discretion to fix the amount of attorney's fees, where the clause uses the word "shall," the court must award fees.[103]

82

---

[101]*3250 Wilshire Blvd. Bldg. v. W.R. Grace & Co.* (9th Cir. 1993) 990 F.2d 487; *Lerner v. Ward* (1993) 13 Cal.App.4th 155; 16 Cal.Rptr.2d 486.

[102]Discussed at pages 9 and 80, *supra.*

[103]*Palmer v. Shawback* (1993) 17 Cal.App.4th 296; 21 Cal.Rptr.2d 575.

C. The Section 1031 Exchange

One of the few tax benefits available since the Tax Reform Act of 1986 is the tax deferred exchange, commonly referred to as the section 1031 exchange. Generally, this section of the Internal Revenue Code permits the trade of one qualifying property for another of "like kind" without paying taxes on the gain from the disposition of the first property, provided that the property taken in trade is equal or greater in value. The justification is that the transaction is really one continuous investment. Occasionally the mechanics of the trade involve a buyer being asked to take title momentarily to a property that the seller wants to acquire in the trade and then exchanging that property for the seller's property.

The seller interested in taking advantage of an exchange wants to be certain that the buyer of his property is going to cooperate. Commonly, when an offer is presented, the seller counters or asks the buyer to execute an addendum providing that *"Buyer agrees to cooperate with Seller in effecting an IRS § 1031 exchange."* Most buyers are willing to sign such a counter or addendum because they are completely unaware of what might be required by way of "cooperation." Then, at the closing, the buyer may be presented with documents whereby he takes title, although only momentarily, to property which he or she has never heard of.

83

A sophisticated buyer will balk at taking title, and for good reason. He or she might, for example, be exposed to liability if the property that he or she is asked to hold title has toxic contamination problems. Although "innocent purchasers" are sometimes protected, the Superfund Acts[104] can involve anyone in the chain of title in extensive litigation to determine who is liable for the cost of cleanup.

If the buyer refuses to accept the transitory title, has the buyer breached the purchase agreement, subjecting him or her to extensive damages because of the adverse tax consequences to the seller if the deal does not go through? Buyer and seller will look to the agents for help, explanations, and perhaps money for not clearly spelling out in what way the buyer had obligated himself or herself to "cooperate." Claims have been made by disappointed sellers where the tax regulations were

---

[104]Federal Comprehensive Environmental Response, Compensation and Liability Act of 1980 (CERCLA) as modified by the Superfund Amendments and Reauthorization Act of 1986 (SARA) and parallel state statutes such as the California Hazardous Substance Act (Health & Safety Code §§25300 *et seq.*).

changed, even though after escrow, rendering the exchange invalid, such as changing the definition of "like kind" property.[105] These potential problems can be avoided if, as a standard practice, the following or similar language, is inserted in the contract:

> **Buyer agrees to accommodate seller in effecting a tax-deferred exchange under Internal Revenue Code §1031. Seller shall have the right, expressly reserved here, to elect this tax-deferred exchange at any time before closing date. Buyer agrees to execute all documents reasonably necessary in connection with such an exchange, provided that:**
>
> > **(a) Buyer shall not be required to take title to any property, real or personal, other than the subject property;**
> >
> > **(b) such cooperation shall not delay the closing date;**
> >
> > **(c) such cooperation shall be at no cost or expense to Buyer; and**
> >
> > **(d) consummation of this agreement is not predicated or conditioned upon the exchange.**
>
> **It is understood that neither the Buyer or the Brokers have given any advice to Seller concerning the exchange or the possible impact of any pending legislation.**

In most cases, the party interested in a 1031 exchange may be better advised to use the services of a "facilitator," which is now allowed under tax regulations.

84

D. The Rule Against Perpetuities

Since most lawyers and judges lack a clear understanding of the Rule Against Perpetuities, it is no surprise that most agents are unfamiliar with the consequences of violating the rule. In a nutshell, the rule is that no interest in property is good unless it must vest, if at all, within 21 years after the death of an individual alive at the creation of the interest.[106] (In legalese, "to vest"

---

[105]Since the agent is not expected to be an expert in tax matters, he or she should not reasonably be expected to give advice about existing tax laws much less changes which are pending but not yet enacted. The cost of defending such claims is, nevertheless, a real possibility.

[106]Calif. Probate Code §21205(a).

means to give the right of enjoyment or use.) Consequently, one finds in older documents, particularly trusts, archaic terminology that the deed must vest "not later than 21 years from the death of the youngest son of the Prince of Wales, successor to the Queen of England, etc." Apparently, great faith was put in the longevity of the British royal family.

California has simplified the matter by providing that the interest is valid if it will vest or terminate "within 90 years after its creation"[107] But the rule can create troublesome consequences. For example, a provision in the purchase agreement that "Escrow shall close on December 15, 1993, or on the sale of Buyer's present home, ..." violates the rule. The sale of the buyer's present home might never occur and therefor the escrow might never close.

Other instances of violations of the rule arise when a promissory note is given in lieu of a cash commission, payable when the property is "resold by buyer"; a lease that is to "commence upon completion of construction"; or a promise to list the property sometime at an unspecified date in the future. Even a provision providing that notice is to be given to the executor of an estate may be invalid since an executor may never be appointed.

85

Fortunately, California courts have taken the sensible approach and uphold provisions which make vesting contingent upon performance within a reasonable time on the ground that a "reasonable time" is ordinarily less than 21 years.[108] Sometimes the court will even insert the phrase "within a reasonable time" into the contract. However, any question can be avoided by simply adding the phrase **"but not later than [date]"** to all contingencies.

RECOMMEND

E. Inspections

While relatively rare a few years ago, today almost every residential transaction involves some inspection of the property by a licensed professional. Pest control, pool, roof, and septic inspections are common. A general inspection of the property by

---

[107]Calif. Probate Code §21205(b).

[108]See *Wong. v. DiGrazia* (1963) 60 Cal.2d 525; 35 Cal.Rptr.241.

a licensed contractor has become a specialty field. A "contractor's inspection" normally results in a written report which can be most helpful to the purchaser. The cost of a contractor's inspection varies, but usually runs between $250 and $500.

The costs of these inspections can be borne in whatever manner the parties negotiate. Customarily, the seller pays for the termite inspection and any inspection required by local ordinance in connection with the sale of property. The buyer normally pays for structural, geological, roof, pool, septic tank, and like inspections. If a survey is appropriate, its cost is often shared.

Inspections can avoid later surprises and ensuing litigation. **Failure of the agents to recommend and even encourage inspections can constitute negligence.** It is not unusual for buyers to decide not to go forward with inspections, or to limit the inspections to a pest control report, due to lack of funds. It is the duty of the agent to advise the buyer that having an appropriate inspection is essential to the purchase. An "as is" sale should never be completed without a contractor's inspection. The fact that a buyer has declined to order inspections after being urged to do so should be noted in the office file.

CAUTION

86

Unless the buyer is experienced in acquiring real property, he or she will ask the agent for recommendations of various persons or companies to perform whatever inspections are appropriate. In one case the agent recommended her brother, a licensed contractor, to perform the inspection. The buyers did not want to pay for the cost of a written report, so they decided to accompany the brother on his inspection and make notes and ask questions as they went along. When stains indicating a roof leak were observed, the seller said they occurred when the building was under construction and, since completed, there had been no leaks. The brother testified that he told the buyers that it would be prudent to obtain a roof inspection to make certain that the seller was correct. The buyers testified that the brother said no such thing. Because he had been recommended by their agent, they assumed he would check the roof as well as the other component parts of the house. As one might suspect, after the buyers took occupancy, the roof leaked like a sieve.

After the jury rendered a substantial verdict in favor of the buyers, the attorneys asked jury members why they chose to believe the buyers over the testimony of the brother-contractor. They responded that given the relationship of the brother to the agent, they felt that he would cover up any defects so that his sister could close the deal and get a commission. In other words, his credibility was in question from the outset.

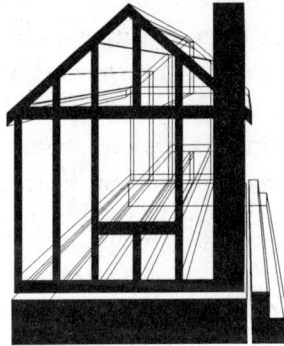

F. The "As Is" Addendum

When a property needs repair — a "fixer upper" — the seller will want to make certain the buyer clearly understands this condition and will not seek redress from the seller for undisclosed defects. There is a general misconception that selling the property "as is" takes care of this concern. This is not true. Civil Code section 1668 provides that all contracts attempting to except anyone from responsibility for fraud or wilful injury, or wilful or negligent violation of the law, are unenforceable. Consequently, the "as is" clause does nothing for the wilful failure to disclose. Intentional or even negligent misrepresentations are not protected.

A contract exempting a party from ordinary negligence is valid. However, a contract that tries to insulate a party from liability for negligent misrepresentation is not enforceable because negligent misrepresentation in California is a form of fraud.[109] The courts hold that "a contract which exempts a party from liability for his own positive assertions, made in a manner not warranted by the information, which are untrue, is against the policy of the law."[110]

87

As a result, the effect of the "as is" provision is limited and often uncertain. Some courts say that the clause merely means **"that the buyer takes the property in the condition which is visible or observable by him."**[111] The phrase does not relieve sellers from the duty to disclose all defects of which they are aware. For example, if the seller has had a termite inspection revealing extensive damage, the seller may not legally conceal the report. The same holds true for past slide conditions or other serious defects not readily observable. Sellers should be cau-

CAUTION ➤

---

[109]1 Miller & Starr, California Real Estate (2d ed. 1989) §1:104, p. 334.

[110]*Blankenhein v. E.F. Hutton & Co.* (1990) 217 Cal.App.3d 1463, 1473; 266 Cal.Rptr. 593, 599.

[111]*Lingsch v. Savage* (1963) 213 Cal.App.2d 729, 742; 29 Cal.Rptr. 201, 209.

tioned that the "as is" provision is no cure-all and does not relieve the seller of the basic duty of disclosure.

Some trial courts have found that in "as is" transactions the purchaser does accept some risks and is responsible for calculating their nature. The "as is" condition puts the purchaser on notice that he or she should have professionals inspect the premises — or be prepared to accept defects those inspections would have revealed, providing they have not been intentionally concealed by the seller.

Regardless of the uncertainty as to the legal effect of "as is" provisions, clearly the inclusion of the phrase has a psychological effect in deterring purchasers from later claiming damages for defects that were perhaps beyond the scope of the purchaser's intended undertaking. A carefully drafted "as is" provision will enhance this psychological deterrent and perhaps save the seller from unjustified claims from a disappointed or frustrated purchaser.

An "as is" clause can be set forth in the purchase agreement under the **Additional Terms and Conditions** paragraph as follows:

This property is being sold in an "AS IS" condition, with no representation or warranty made concerning its condition. Purchasers acknowledge that they have been cautioned to obtain inspections from qualified professionals as to the condition of the property, and have agreed to accept the property in an "as is" and "where is" condition. This provision supersedes all other provisions in this agreement regarding maintenance prior to close of escrow.

88

It is prudent to cross out the maintenance provision of the purchase agreement to make certain that the contract does not contain contradictory provisions. However, questions often arise about physical conditions that deteriorate between the time the buyer completes the inspection and the close of escrow. For this reason, and also to spell out the meaning more fully, the preferable practice is to attach an Addendum to the contract which sets forth the "as is" condition in more detail. A sample is attached as an Appendix B.

RECOMMEND ▶

The Court of Appeals recently reviewed an "as is" provision and added an interesting twist. In *Loughrin v. Superior Court*[112] the seller contended that the "as is" addendum constitutes a waiver of the disclosure requirements of Civil Code section 1102

---

[112](1993) 15 Cal.App.4th 1188; 19 Cal.Rptr.2d 161.

(the Transfer Disclosure Statement). It was argued that the seller could not be held liable for checking the "NO" box to some of the questions even though, given his experience with the property, he should have known better. The trial court agreed with the seller and granted summary judgment in his favor.

The Court of Appeal reversed this judgment. It said that since the requirement of the property disclosure statement does not involve a "public interest," a *"knowing and explicit waiver of the benefits of section 1102 et seq. can be effective."* It held, however, that the standard "as is" clause does not constitute such a waiver, particularly since other printed provisions in the purchase agreement state that the seller will provide the TDS and the seller actually does furnish the form. The court concluded that the seller can avoid claims based upon defects he did not discover because of lack of inspection, but he cannot avoid claims based on inadvertence or forgetfulness in filling out the transfer disclosure form. **To avoid supplying the TDS, the "as is" addendum must specifically waive the provisions of Civil Code section 1102.**

An "As Is Addendum" containing a TDS waiver is included in Appendix C. The seller still has to disclose any defects of which he or she is aware. These distinctions sometimes become subtle, and care should be taken to carefully explain them so that the seller is fully aware of his or her responsibilities. If you use the expanded "As Is Addendum," be sure to line out the printed contract provision that the seller is to furnish a TDS. **The use of an "as is" addendum that waives the TDS on the part of the seller should be used cautiously and only under compelling circumstances.** For example, it might be used where the seller has never occupied the property and has no knowledge of its condition.

CAUTION

89

While the decision in the *Loughrin* case refers to "the parties [and] their real estate representatives," it would seem that, even with the expanded "As Is Addendum," the agents still need to make and report on the TDS the results of the required visual inspection, particularly since this is mandated under a different statute (Civil Code § 2079) which might well not be subject to waiver.[113] One solution would be to strike out Parts I and II

---

[113]This issue was raised but not decided in *Wilson v. Century 21 Great Western Realty* (1993) 15 Cal.App.4th 298; 18 Cal.Rptr.2d 779, where the court said: ". . . it appears to be an open question whether an 'as is' provision in a realty sales contract validly relieves the broker of negligence liability for failure to discharge inspect-and-disclose duties owed to a buyer

of the transfer disclosure form and note "**Waived — As Is Sale**," and answer Parts III and IV, the agents' disclosure sections.

G. Non-refundable Deposits

90

Often when the Buyer asks for more time to make inspections, obtain financing, or extend some other contingency in the purchase agreement, the Seller will ask, in exchange for the extension, that the deposit, or a portion of it, become "non-refundable." Frequently, neither the parties nor the agents recognize that such a provision is in fact a "**liquidated damage**" clause subject to all the statutory provisions governing liquidated damages. The non-refundable deposit is simply a forfeiture to be suffered by the buyer if he does not complete the transaction.

When the purchase agreement involves the sale of residential real property involving four units or less, liquidated damages are presumed to be unreasonable if they exceed three percent (3%) of the sale price. In addition, in order to be enforceable, the provision must be initialed by both parties.[114] Unfortunately, when couched in the language of a "non-refundable deposit," the parties often ignore these requirements. There is nothing wrong with the use of "non-refundable" deposits, providing that the rules regarding liquidated damages are applied. While the three percent rule does not apply to commercial or raw land sales, it is important to remember that even in these sales the provisions for liquidated damages is invalid unless separately signed or initialled by each party to the contract.[115]

---

under section 2079 (see also § 1102 et seq.). We need not decide the question as the evidence here does not show a breach of statutory obligations."

[114]Calif. Civil Code §1675.

[115]Calif. Civil Code §1677.

H. Maintenance Provisions

Most standard purchase agreements contain a provision obligating the seller to maintain the various systems and appliances of the home in good working order until the close of escrow. For example, Professional Publishing Form No. 101-R.1 CAL (1-93) provides in ¶27 as follows:

> **MAINTENANCE.** Seller covenants that the heating, air-conditioning (if any), electrical, solar, septic system, gutter and downspout, sprinkler (if any), and plumbing systems including the water heater, pool and spa systems, as well as built-in appliances and other mechanical apparatus shall be in working order on the date possession is delivered. Seller shall replace any cracked or broken glass including windows, mirrors, shower and tub enclosures. Until possession is delivered Seller shall maintain all structures, landscaping, grounds and pool (if any). Seller agrees to deliver the property in a neat and clean condition with all debris and personal belongings removed. The following items are specifically excluded from the above:

If the property disclosure statement reveals, for example, that the sprinkler system does not function properly, is the seller relieved of his obligation, under the maintenance provision of the agreement quoted above, to repair the defect prior to close of escrow? There are no cases that directly address the problem, and a credible argument can be made that the handwritten portion of the property disclosure statement takes precedence over the printed provision under the general rule that in case of conflict or ambiguity the written provisions of a contract control.[116]

The Professional Publishing form attempts to resolve this problem in the paragraph relating to the property disclosure statement by providing:

> Buyer and Seller understand that no provision in the RETDS, and/or any supplement or addendum, obligates the Seller to correct or improve the condition of items disclosed, however, Seller shall not be relieved of his obligation under item 27, MAINTENANCE, or any of the INSPECTION CLAUSES in item 36.

If the form you use does not have such a clarifying provision, whenever a defect is disclosed in the property disclosure statement, an addendum to the contract should be prepared providing as follows:

---

[116]Calif. Civil Code §1651.

91

The fact that a defect is disclosed in the property disclosure statement or by inspection shall not relieve the seller from the responsibility to correct said defect if otherwise provided in the purchase agreement.

Also not resolved by the case law is the situation where the property disclosure statement does not indicate any defects in the operating systems, but the buyers, conducting their inspections, discover one or more systems (such as the pool heater, for example) are not working and need repair. This can easily happen when the premises are not owner-occupied. Can the buyer sandbag the seller and not mention the defective pool heater? Then, immediately after escrow, tell the sellers that they are obligated under the maintenance clause to furnish the buyers a pool heater in working order?

A literal reading of most maintenance clauses seems to indicate that buyers, however sleazy their conduct, could get away with keeping the defect secret until after escrow closes. This seems particularly true where the agreement provides that mere disclosure of a defect in an operating system in the property disclosure statement does not relieve the sellers of the duty to repair. A vast difference separates these two situations, however. Where the sellers are aware of the non-operational system, they can specifically exclude it from the maintenance provision. If they are unaware it exists, they have no such option. Under these circumstances it seems to the author that the buyers must reveal the non-operational system to the sellers and negotiate for its repair. Otherwise, the buyers are breaching the covenant of good faith and fair dealing implied in all contracts.

RECOMMEND

The procedure recommended by many brokers who have addressed this problem is to have the buyers categorize all defects discovered in the inspection process as either maintenance items (appliances, pool, plumbing, electrical, etc.) or as structural and site defect items (roof, drainage, soil conditions, and the like). Sellers should be notified that they are expected to put maintenance items in good working order by the time escrow closes. Items not included in the maintenance clause are subject to negotiation. If the seller refuses either or both proposals, the buyers have the option of terminating the agreement.

Of course, if the systems or appliances were found in good working order at the time of inspection, it is the sellers' responsibility to maintain them in good working order until the close of escrow.

I. Back-up Offers

One of the first signs that a down real estate market is reviving are multiple offers on the same property. While this may make the seller very confident, it can be a serious trap for the unwary. In the mid-1980s there were many lawsuits by buyers claiming that the seller had sold the same property twice.

There are two situations which most often trigger complaints by the back-up buyer. First, the seller must be careful that the first contract is really terminated before putting the back-up offer in primary position. Often when the time for performance by the first buyer expires, the seller believes that he or she is in a position to proceed with the back-up proposal. However, the failure to perform on the part of the first buyer may be legally excused or, as is often the case, the first buyer will claim that the seller did not fully tender performance, and the buyer's right to purchase has not been effectively terminated. To avoid this result, it is important that the secondary agreement contain language that it is not effective until the primary buyer confirms in writing that the first deal is dead. Written instructions cancelling the first escrow signed by both the parties is the easiest way of accomplishing this result.

CAUTION

The second trap occurs when the seller and the primary buyer modify the terms of the first contract. Technically, under the provisions of the back-up offer, the seller promises to convey the property if the first offer is not consummated **according to its terms.** If the parties change the terms of the first deal, for example, by increasing the purchase price, altering the amount of the down payment, or extending the time for closing, the secondary offeror can legitimately claim that he or she is now in first position. To avoid this result, the secondary agreement should contain language that permits the parties to the primary agreement to modify its terms.

CAUTION

While some pre-printed forms attempt to include sections dealing with back-up offers, it is recommended that they be addressed by language in the "other terms and provisions" section of the form or by a simple addendum. The frequency of back-up offers does not justify it being included as a standard provision. Moreover, the nature of back-up offers requires some flexibility in the language used. Be careful to insert a termination

93

date to avoid violations of the rule against perpetuities.[117] The back-up offer must either become effective or terminate on or before a date certain.

The following language can be easily modified to fit the particular situation:

BACK-UP OFFER ADDENDUM

Buyer and Seller acknowledge that a primary agreement now exists on the subject property, and that this agreement is accepted in a secondary or back-up position under the following terms and conditions:

1. **This contract shall become primary upon termination of the existing primary agreement. Termination does not occur until the primary offeror executes written cancellation instructions.**

2. **Until Buyer has received written notice the prior agreement has been terminated and this contract is in primary position:**

   (a) **Buyer may terminate this contract, without liability, by giving written notice to Seller or Seller's agent;**

   (b) **All time periods specified here will not begin to run;**

   (c) **Buyer need not open escrow or tender the down payment.**

3. **Seller reserves the right to extend or modify any and all terms and conditions of the primary agreement at Seller's discretion.**

4. **Unless placed in primary position within _____ days from the date hereof, this agreement shall terminate and be of no further force and effect.**

J. How Should the Buyer Take Title?

94

Often a Purchase Agreement contains a provision asking the buyer to specify how title to the property will be taken, i.e., as joint tenants, community property, or something else. Some agreements wisely state that the manner of taking title may have significant tax consequences, and the buyer should seek advice from an accountant or lawyer before deciding. In any event, this decision need not be made by the buyer until shortly before the

---

[117]See page 84, *supra.*

escrow instructions are ready to sign, at which time the title company will ask how the deed is to be prepared.

A competent agent should be familiar enough with the various ways in which title can be taken so that he or she can discuss the matter intelligently with the buyer. The most common ways to vest title to residential property are as follows:

1. Joint Tenants

A **joint tenancy** conveyance is made to two or more persons in equal shares. The primary characteristic of joint tenancy is that on the death of one co-owner, a right of survivorship accrues to the remaining joint tenants, which removes the property from the decedent's estate.[118] This means a joint tenant has no power to dispose of his or her interest by will. There may also be significant tax disadvantages in joint tenancy ownership. For example, on the death of one joint tenant, only that tenant's interest gets a stepped-up basis for tax purposes. In community property, the entire property gets a new basis on the death of one of the owners. Joint tenancy is not recommended unless special circumstances warrant it. A joint tenancy can be terminated during the life of the joint tenants if one of them conveys his interest to another or himself as tenant in common. This can be done without the consent of the other joint tenant.

95

2. Tenants in Common

In a **tenancy in common**, each tenant enjoys a separate but undivided interest in the property. This interest can be conveyed by deed or by a will.[119] Unlike joint tenancy, the undivided interests of tenants in common need not be equal. For example, one person may own an undivided 25 percent interest and the other a 75 percent interest. Each tenant has an estate that, on death, passes to his or her heirs or under his or her will if the tenant in common has one, rather than to the surviving tenants in common. This form of ownership is often used in "equity sharing" arrangements where the rights and duties of each tenant in common are set forth in a "Tenancy in Common Agreement."

3. Community Property

Community property is a form of co-ownership applicable only to property owned by a husband and wife during their marriage to each other. Each spouse may dispose of his or her one-half share of the community property by will. However, if

---

[118]*Estate of England* (1991) 233 Cal.App.3d 1; 284 Cal.Rptr. 361.

[119]*Estate of England* (1991) *supra*, footnote 118.

there is no will, or if the surviving spouse is a beneficiary under the will, the administration of probate proceedings may be avoided by filing a simple "spousal petition" with the probate court. This type of ownership has many tax advantages and is usually recommended by estate planners.

Community property is normally all property that has been acquired during the marriage by a person while domiciled in California, unless acquired with separate property. "Separate property" is generally all the property of either spouse owned before marriage or acquired afterward by gift or inheritance. Spouses, by written agreement, can change community property into separate property and *vice-versa*. Community property is ordinarily divided equally between the parties in the event of divorce, so care should be exercised in transforming separate property into community property. Transfers between spouses are normally exempt from income, gift, or capital gains taxes.

4. Combinations

Title can be taken by combining one or more of the above types of ownership. For example, "A conveys Blackacre to B, as a tenant in common, as to an undivided one-third interest, and to C and D, as joint tenants, as to an undivided two-thirds interest."

Part V
Dual Agency

A. The Agency Relationship

"An inflexible rule of law declares that an agent vested with discretionary authority cannot represent two parties having conflicting interests without the principal's prior consent or subsequent ratification after full disclosure of all the facts" — *Judge Gary Larson, Dismuke v Edina Realty, Inc. (June 21, 1993) No. 92-8716 District Court of Hennepin County, Minnesota.*

To understand the problems and challenges involved in dual agency, it is necessary to briefly review the agency relationships in real estate transactions *vis á vis* the salesperson and the seller and buyer. Real estate agents and brokers would like to believe they are independent contractors whose function is to bring a buyer and seller together in a non-adversarial situation. One advocate in the field urges that the agency concept, with all of its hangups and conflicts, is a creature of lawyers who "must play a win/lose game, similar to a sports contest." Real estate salespeople, on the other hand, "negotiate between the buyer and the seller until we arrive at a win/win situation . . . ."[120] According to this author, the agency concept should be banned from the real estate industry, and salespersons should be known as "real estate facilitator," or, better yet, "real estate brokers." The word "agent" with all of its burdensome fiduciary connotations, would be abandoned.

While this may sell in some jurisdictions, in California the statutory scheme clearly makes a person who participates in any way in the negotiation of a real estate transaction an agent of the party he or she is representing. That person is subject to the statutory and common law rules of agency as well as requirements imposed upon real estate licensees. While the licensee has a duty to act fairly and honestly to all parties to the transaction,

97

---

[120]Irv Also, *Independent Contractor: The Alternate to Real Estate Agency* (Third Rev. Ed. May, 1993); P.O. Box 26150, Tempe, Arizona 85285 (602-730-1423).

he or she is in a fiduciary relationship to the licensee's principal and owes that principal the highest duty of loyalty, honesty, and undivided service. In addition to these fiduciary obligations, the licensee has a duty to use reasonable care and skill in the transaction. These are two separate duties. The first, the fiduciary duty, is owed only to the agent's principal. The second duty of using skill, that is, **acting within the Standard of Care**, applies to agents for both the buyer and the seller. The nature of these duties is spelled out in the statutory agency disclosure form.[121] The use of the agency disclosure form is mandated for residential sales (property improved with one to four dwelling units) but not for commercial transactions. **However, the definitions and statements of duties contained in the form apply to both types of transactions, and it is considered prudent to use the disclosure form in all types of transactions.**

RECOMMEND

There used to be a great deal of confusion as to the role of the cooperating broker when property was listed with the Multiple Listing Service. Did he or she become the agent of the seller? Since the cooperating broker also represented the buyer, was he or she a dual agent? Exploring these relationships can cause severe headache — authoritative explanations are incomprehensible to all but the serious student of the law.[122] Suffice it to say that appropriate use of the agency disclosure form with its explanations ordinarily shields the agent from attack in this regard, at least in those areas where dual agency is not involved.

Dual agency arises when one broker represents both seller and buyer — as when the agent sells his or her own listing. In smaller offices, the listing agent typically announces the listing at an office meeting, hoping that another agent in the same office will have a buyer. In large firms, one branch commonly sells the listing of an agent in another branch or city. These are all dual agency situations.

Dual agency is actually invited by many sellers. They list their property with a particular agent expecting him or her to "sell" the property. The practice of dual agency has been recognized by the courts for years and was specifically recognized by the legislature when it enacted the mandatory agency disclosure

98

---

[121]Calif. Civil Code §2375.

[122]See, *e.g.*, the explanation of "Subagents" in the California Department of Real Estate, Reference Book (1989-90 ed.) pp. 203-204.

form. The form provides: "A real estate agent either acting directly or through one or more associate licensees, can legally be the agent of both the Seller and the Buyer in a transaction, but only with the knowledge and consent of both the Seller and the Buyer." With such explicit approval one might reasonably ask, What is the problem? The problem is that when an agent is in a fiduciary relationship to his principal, he or she owes the duty of undivided service to that principal.[123] How can one give undivided service to two principals?

B. The Levels of Conflict

One of the first questions, of course, is how an agent representing both the buyer and seller can advocate pricing strategies with either party without violating the agent's trust with the other. The disclosure form attempts to handle this major conflict by simply providing the following rule:

> In representing both Seller and Buyer, the agent may not, without the express permission of the respective party, disclose to the other party that the Seller will accept a price less than the listing price or that the Buyer will pay a price greater than the price offered.

99

This effectively cuts off the agent from giving any advice at all regarding price negotiations in offers and counteroffers. Any suggestion about what should be offered or countered would justifiably concern the principals that their confidences were being compromised. Accepting a dual agent eliminates the use of the agent's assistance and skill in this regard.

What about other facets of the transaction such as the condition of the property, inspections, financing, terms, the financial ability of the buyer in seller carry-back financing, the need of the seller to unload (the so-called "motivated" seller), and a dozen other matters. Can one person effectively represent both parties in dealing with all of these items?

The scholars in the field conclude nearly unanimously that dual representation is like having no representation at all. For example, Miller and Starr in their exhaustive treatise, conclude that "the disclosure of the relationship does not resolve the schizophrenic obligations of the broker. The duty of a licensee

---

[123]*Gann v. Williams Brothers Realty, Inc.* (1991) 231 Cal.App.3d 1698; 283 Cal.Rptr. 128.

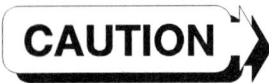

when acting as the agent of the seller is to negotiate for the sale of the property at the highest price and for the best terms for the seller. The duty of a licensee when acting as the agent for the buyer is to obtain the lowest price and a purchase of the property for the best terms for the buyer. These duties are, almost by definition, completely contradictory. They cannot be performed at the same time or in the course of the same transaction by the licensee without creating the danger that the rights of one of the principals will be sacrificed to promote the interests of the other, or that neither principal will receive the benefits otherwise obtained by a full and faithful exercise of the licensee's fiduciary duties."[124]

The degree of the conflict of interest varies considerably depending upon the factual situation. If the agent representing the seller operates out of a different branch than the agent representing the buyer, the negotiations are at least subject to two competing agents and are being reviewed and supervised by two different managers. While this is still a dual agency because of the common broker of record, it provides almost, if not all, the protections and negotiating skills that are available to the parties when represented by two different brokers.

When both agents operate out of the same office, the conflict becomes greater, but at least features two different persons advising the parties. It is when one person represents both parties that the conflict becomes irreconcilable and the schizophrenic situation alluded to in Miller & Starr is present.

The most unacceptable situation arises when the agent is acting on his or her own account as a seller and, desiring to participate fully in the commission, also represents the buyer. This practice is actually encouraged by some brokers. It is inconceivable that the buyer has even a remote chance of being adequately represented and, if ever a complaint arises in such a situation, it is promptly settled out of court. There is no justification, legal or moral, for such a practice.

Some agents "avoid the conflict" by referring the selling end to another agent in the office, and taking the "usual" twenty-five percent referral fee. Such a referral fee probably makes the other agent a sub-agent of the agent-seller, if that relationship has not already been established because of the common supervising broker. While the referral method is the best way to handle the

100

CAUTION

---

[124] 2 Miller & Starr, California Real Estate (2d ed. 1989) *Agency* §3:8, p. 46.

RECOMMEND

conflict, it should be a referral to another brokerage, and there should be no referral fee. While this may seem a severe solution, the reciprocity that good agents use will soon put you on the receiving end of such a referral relationship. You will gain in the long run.

C. Protective Devices

The law provides that dual agency is legal if the parties "knowingly consent" to it. The statutory agency disclosure statement goes a long way towards informing the parties so that their knowing consent can be established. However, as with all printed forms, without explanation the provisions are usually never read or, if read, poorly comprehended. When the agency disclosure form is presented for signature, a brief oral explanation of the form is appropriate. A note should be kept in the file that such an explanation was given and that the party involved was encouraged to read the form carefully. The California Association of Realtors Legal Department has published an "Agency Disclosure Law Compliance Manual"[125] which sets forth a three-step procedure to assure compliance with the agency disclosure law. Though perhaps overly detailed, the manual, in a question and answer format, is a comprehensive explanation of the law and its application in various situations.

101

More important, if there is to be dual agency, a complete and thorough explanation should be given when the confirmation section is completed, whether this be in the contract of sale, the separate confirmation form, or both. A note should be made in the agent's file that such an explanation was made and that the parties appeared to understand. As an extra precaution, some brokers require that the parties execute a specific "Consent to Dual Agency," a copy of which is included as Appendix D. This form, short and to the point, should remove any doubt that the consent was given "knowingly." Professional Publishing Corporation also provides a "Dual Agency Disclosure Addendum," Form 100-DA, which serves the same purpose.

CAUTION

---

[125]Available from the California Association of Realtors order desk at 213-739-8227.

D. The Future of Dual Agency

The more objective observers in the real estate industry predict that dual agency will not be with us long. The evidence supports this conclusion. It was not long ago that attorneys felt no compunction in representing both the husband and wife in an uncontested divorce. In *Klemm v. Superior Court (County of Fresno)*,[126] the Court confirmed there can be dual representation "where there is a full disclosure and informed consent by all the parties. . . ." However, it went on to hold that, *as a matter of law,* a purported consent to dual representation where there are adverse interests at a contested hearing can be neither intelligent nor informed. It said: ". . . common sense dictates that it would be unthinkable to permit an attorney to assume a position at a trial or hearing where he could not advocate the interest of one client without adversely injuring those of the other."

After this case, it became rare indeed for one attorney to attempt to represent both parties in a dissolution proceeding.

The same principles apply in real estate transactions. The licensee is hired, not only to bring a buyer and seller together, but because he or she has certain skills and training that are relied upon by the parties to protect their respective interests. The question is whether, assuming full disclosure, "informed consent" is possible.

A case in point is recently settled litigation in Minneapolis. A class action suit was brought by two sellers against the well-known Edina Realty, Inc. for acting as dual agents in real estate transactions.[127] Edina, the state's second-largest broker (1700 agents and 42 offices), has permitted dual agency transactions since the Minnesota legislature, in 1986, permitted dual agency with "affirmative written disclosure."[128] Edina's competitor, Burnet Realty, Inc., the state's largest broker (1850 agents and 39 offices) has discouraged the practice among its agents. The trial court held that, while the language in the purchase agreement purporting to explain dual agency satisfied the statutory

102

---

[126](1977) 75 Cal.App.3d 893, 898; 142 Cal.Rptr. 509, 512.

[127]*Dismuke v. Edina Realty, Inc.,* No. 92-8716, Hennepin County District Court, Minnesota.

[128]Minn. State. Sec. 82.19, subd. 5 provides in pertinent part: "(a) No person licensed pursuant to this chapter . . . shall represent any party or parties to a real estate transaction . . . unless the person makes an affirmative written disclosure to all parties to the transaction as to which party that person represents in the transaction. The disclosure shall be printed in at least 6 point bold type on the purchase agreement and acknowledged by separate signatures of the buyer and seller."

disclosure obligation, "it cannot be characterized as either full or adequate disclosure of all the facts under common law." The language used in the contract was as follows:

Agency Disclosure: _____(selling agent) stipulated he or she is representing the _____in this transaction. The listing agent or broker stipulates he or she is representing the seller in this transaction. Buyer and seller initial: Buyer(s)_____ Seller(s) _____

This is obviously not a very informative disclosure, and the court found that its use constituted a breach of fiduciary duty. It ordered a refund of commissions to an estimated 30,000 sellers which would cost Edina Realty $210 million.

A Federal suit under the Racketeer Influence and Corrupt Organizations Act (RICO) was also filed in which both buyers and sellers are suing Edina alleging fraud, breach of fiduciary duty, as well as violations of the RICO act.[129] The federal court permitted this suit to proceed as a class action for the benefit of both the sellers and the buyers on the theory that a jury could find that the commission is in fact paid out of the transaction by both parties to the buy-sell agreement. This novel approach is, of course, contrary to the traditional view that the seller alone is the one who pays the commission, absent a buyer-broker agreement. Since triple damages are awarded under RICO violations, Edina faced another $630 million in damages.

103

It is reported that the Edina cases have been settled for a payment of $21 million. Not something that your ordinary brokerage could readily handle. The case is a good example of the consequences of not using "plain language" forms.

Realtors in California claim that since the legislature in California specifically authorized dual agency, there is no chance of an Edina-type result. Not so. If there are situations in which "informed consent" cannot, *as a matter of law,* be given, then the agency disclosure would be found to be in violation of the common law rule even though it might technically comply with the statute regarding agency disclosure. The statute would simply be found insufficient to protect a buyer's or seller's right to an uncompromised fiduciary relationship. The action by the court would probably be prospective only, that is, apply only to future cases. However, it would most likely be couched in language to send a clear signal that no matter what kind of disclosure is

---

[129]*Bokusky et al. v. Edina Realty, Inc. et al.*, U.S. Dist. Court, Minnesota, 3rd Div., No. 3-92 CIV 223.

made or acknowledged by the principals, under all but a few factual circumstances dual agency is inappropriate and prohibited as a matter of law. The statute might even be held to violate the constitutional right to due process of law and therefore invalid as applied to most situations.

Realtors argue that any action outlawing dual agency would devastate the real estate industry, particularly the large brokers who like to control both the listing and selling ends of the transaction. But how did the Burnett Realty in Minneapolis do so well when it prohibited dual agency transactions? The lawyers prohibited from representing both parties in divorces managed to survive. The impact would probably be far less severe than is feared, and it would certainly restore the confidence of the consumers in the real estate industry.

Avoid dual agency situations whenever possible. Half of a commission is better than risking having to return the whole commission. If dual agency is unavoidable, cover yourself by providing "informed consent" to the highest degree possible.

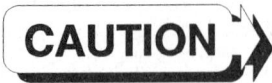

CAUTION

104

Part VI
Creative Financing

Whenever the residential real estate market slows down, a number of "sales tools" appear that, in more prosperous times, would be frowned upon. While some of these devices are legitimate efforts to move properties which sellers desperately wish to unload, others constitute fraud, or more charitably, gross negligence on the part of the participating agent.

A. Seller Carryback Financing

CAUTION

Take for example the "cash-to-buyer" or "buyer walk-away" transactions prevalent during the slow markets of 1980-1981 and again in 1984. Despite warnings from the Department of Real Estate in its quarterly Real Estate Bulletin, many agents were duped into thinking this was legitimate "creative financing." Seminars conducted throughout the state on purchasing property with "no money down" failed to point out that the seller was often the victim in such transactions.

A typical example of this type of creative financing can be found in the story of Earl and Mary Baker, retired government employees.[130] Their residence in Novato was worth about $130,000. A small first deed of trust of approximately $10,000 was owed against the property. Mary Baker contacted a friend, Pat, an agent at a well-known brokerage. She wanted to use the substantial equity in the property to construct a retirement home at Lake Tahoe. Pat had attended a lecture by an agent of a mortgage loan broker on the subject of creative financing. Without any prior experience, Pat suggested to the Bakers that, with the slow market, creative financing was the best way to go.

The scheme structured called for Tim, the loan agent who had given the lecture, to purchase the Baker home for $130,000. A new three-year first deed of trust in the amount of $80,000 was arranged by Tim through his employer, a private loan

105

---

[130] The facts are taken from the case of *Baker v. Breen, et al.*, Marin County Superior Court No. 107338, concerning a transaction occurring in October, 1980.

brokerage firm. The note carried an 18 percent interest rate and was due in three years. The Bakers carried back a purchase-money second deed of trust in the amount of $74,800. The following disbursements were made from the new first deed of trust:

Taxes	$ 500
Pay off existing first	10,000
Commission (split 2/3 to Pat; 1/3 to Tim)	6,500
Points to Loan Broker for new first	10,500
To Purchaser Tim (ostensibly for repairs)	12,500
To Sellers	38,000
	$80,000

At the close of escrow, the total encumbrances against the property, including the purchase money second taken back by the Bakers, totalled $154,800.

No repairs were made by Tim, the purchaser. He promptly defaulted on both the first and second, and then filed bankruptcy. His former employer foreclosed on the first and was the only bidder at the foreclosure sale. The Bakers claimed that, having used the cash they received to make a down payment on the Tahoe house, they had no funds available to cure the default.

Of course, Tim wore many hats during the transaction. He was the buyer, the agent at the brokerage house that arranged the loan, and an agent in the sales transaction, working for his own account. Pat was in a fiduciary relationship and was accused of (1) failing to investigate the financial ability of the buyer to perform on the carry-back second deed of trust, and (2) failing to advise the Bakers of the risks involved when the encumbrances at the close of escrow exceeded the fair market value of the house. The brokers for both Tim and Pat were responsible for their negligence and, in the case of Tim, his broker was responsible for what a jury could justifiably find as fraudulent conduct.

Pat's broker tendered her a defense under her Independent Associate Agreement, but Tim's broker, though named as a defendant, adamantly refused to accept any responsibility, claiming that it only made the loan. Tim, of course, was in bankruptcy and supposedly had no funds to contribute to a settlement. Shortly before the trial commenced, the loan broker decided the risk was too great and agreed to contribute to a settlement. The plaintiff accepted $41,500 from Pat's broker and $31,500 from Tim's broker as a final settlement. In consideration of the settlement, the Bakers waived their right to recover attorney fees and costs.

The Department of Real Estate has listed the five characteristics of this type of transaction. They are:

✓ The buyer invests none of his own money.

✓ The buyer arranges for a new first or second loan to finance the purchase.

✓ The seller carries back a large junior note and deed of trust from the buyer.

✓ The encumbrances against the property represented by the buyer's note and senior encumbrances exceed the fair market value of the property.

✓ The seller agrees to the buyer receiving part of the cash from the new loan.

Effective July 1, 1983, the California legislature enacted Civil Code sections 2956-2967. These sections require that the licensee (called the "arranger of credit") deliver a Seller Financing Disclosure Statement detailing the creative financing scheme. While helpful, the statement may not sufficiently alert the unsophisticated seller.

If your transaction involves the elements listed above, or most of them, take time to carefully analyze the deal to make certain your client is not being defrauded. If there is any question, insist that the seller's attorney approve the transaction in writing. Failure to take these precautionary steps could lead to the loss of your license and disastrous financial consequences.

CAUTION

107

B. The Installment Land Contract

108

In the early 1980s, when the market was slow and loans were not readily assumable, the installment land contract became a popular sales tool. In using this device, the seller retains title until the purchase price has been paid in full. Rather than using the terms "seller" and "buyer," the parties are designated "vendor" and "vendee." The contract calls for the vendee to make a down payment, usually modest, and then agrees to make monthly payments equal to the payments owing under the first deed of trust note and second deed of trust note, if there is one. The balance of the purchase price is paid in amortized monthly installments, usually being fully paid off between five to ten years. When paid off, the vendee receives title and has the option of assuming the balance of the existing loans or refinancing. The vendee customarily takes possession of the premises during the life of the contract and is required to maintain it and pay all taxes and other carrying costs the same as if having legal title.

The form usually gives the parties the option of having the vendee pay the monthly payments on the underlying loans directly to the lender or, more frequently, to the vendor who is then responsible for making payments on the underlying deeds of trust. Whatever means is chosen, there is always apprehension about whether the party responsible for making the mortgage payments will faithfully keep them current. Various devices are employed to try to give the parties some assurance in this regard. Sometimes it is agreed the monthly payments are to be made to an independent third party, but this device often proves to be expensive and cumbersome. The problem was greatly alleviated by enactment of sections 2920(b) and 2924(e) of the Civil Code permitting the vendor (with the consent of the vendee) to request a notice of all delinquencies of four months or more from beneficiaries of the underlying deeds of trust.

The installment land contract has long been popular in the Midwest where it is referred to as a "contract for deed." The major problem with its use there is the lack of a speedy and inexpensive method for the seller to clear the title to the property in the event of default by the vendee. While the vendor retains legal title, the vendee acquires, by virtue of the agreement and his payments under it, an equitable interest in the property. To obtain clear title in the event of default, the vendor is obliged to pursue a quiet title action in court. Sometimes the parties seek to avoid this problem by each executing a quitclaim deed to a third party escrow holder with instructions that if the buyer is in default the buyer's deed is to be delivered to the seller, and, if for some reason the seller fails to deliver title to the buyer when the buyer has made all the required payments, the seller's deed can be recorded. The obvious flaw in this arrangement is that absent a court finding, the escrow holder is exposed to all sorts of damages if he or she mistakenly delivers the deed.

Stewart Title Company in California proposed a solution to this problem which quickly gained acceptance from most of the other title companies. It created a form of installment land contract containing a power of sale similar to the one present in a standard deed of trust. As in a deed of trust, it provides that the execution of the installment land contract constitutes a conveyance by both the vendor and vendee of the property to the title company for the purpose of securing the obligations of both the vendor and vendee under the agreement. The agreement sets forth in detail how, in the event of default, a notice of default will be filed and a sale held by the trustee, copying verbatim the California procedure for a power of sale in deeds of trust. If the vendee meets the payment obligations provided for in the agreement, a deed is executed by both the vendor and the trustee conveying legal title to the vendee.

This device became moot when loans became more readily assumable, and taking carry-back second deeds of trust was held not to justify acceleration of the first deed of trust by the underlying lender. However, with loan qualification becoming more difficult, requests for installment land contracts are becoming more frequent. Some title companies will still insure this type of security device. If used properly, they have a legitimate purpose.

109

The installment land contract forms have not been updated in many years and do not contain the various amendments made to the mortgage foreclosure sections of the Civil Code. If the parties want to use an installment land contract, it is highly recommended that the form be completed and explained to them by their attorneys. The complexities and lack of general use of this device remove it from the expertise and training of most real estate agents. Attempting to utilize it without professional legal assistance can lead to serious consequences. Indeed, the Department of Real Estate cautions that filling out forms that "are not commonplace in the ordinary conduct of the agent's business. . . . may very well involve the unlawful practice of law."[131]

CAUTION

---

[131]California Department of Real Estate, *Reference Book* (1989-1990) p. 619.

C. Equity Sharing Arrangements

Equity sharing is a form of joint ownership where a number of individuals own the real property as tenants in common. It is often used in commercial transactions where, for a variety of reasons, the parties do not want to establish a corporation or a partnership to hold title. In this context it is a very useful device. The rights and duties of the joint owners are spelled out in a tenancy in common agreement. If there are several tenants in common, usually a few will be selected as the managing tenants in common to run the day-to-day affairs involving the property.

Unlike joint tenancy, each of the tenants may sell his or her interest or dispose of the interest by will. There is no automatic right of survivorship in the remaining tenants in common. In addition, the interests may be unequal, whereas in a joint tenancy each joint tenant must own an equal share. Absent an agreement to the contrary, each tenant in common has a right to use all of the property, even though he may only have a small undivided interest. Since it is usually difficult for a tenant in common to sell an undivided share, a tenant in common has the right to have his interest partitioned or, if it cannot be physically divided, to force a sale under court supervision. This is called a "partition action."

110

1. Family Sharing

When used in residential property, the tenancy in common arrangement is most successful in family situations. For example, a parent wishing to provide a child with a down payment might well want to take an undivided interest in the property so that the parent can get repaid from a future sale. Or, in the case of a subsequent divorce, a tenant in common parent has considerable say about the property's disposal.

Tenancy in common arrangements are also popular with unmarried couples living together. Without the benefit of an agreement specifying their rights and obligations, in the event of a split, the separation can become very nasty. Experience shows that when the rights of the parties are discussed and reduced to writing in the harmonious environment present at the time of purchase, there is rarely any difficulty in executing those agreements at the time of separation. Absent an agreement, the emotional trauma associated with separation often leads to acrimony and unnecessary disputes concerning the disposition of the property.

There are no set rules about what a tenancy in common agreement should contain. Normally such an agreement:

▶ (1) recites the contributions each party makes to the acquisition;

▶ (2) specifies the percent of undivided interest each party is to own;

▶ (3) spells out who has the right of occupancy and under what conditions;

▶ (3) identifies who is responsible for paying the mortgage, taxes, insurance, and other carrying costs (and entitled to take any resulting tax write-off);

▶ (4) specifies who can make improvements to the premises, under what circumstances, and if the cost of the improvements can be recaptured on resale;

▶ (5) spells out what happens in the event the person responsible for making the payments defaults;

▶ (6) sets forth when the property is to be sold and how the selling price will be determined;

▶ (7) provides for what happens in the event of the death of any of the parties; and, finally,

▶ (8) provides for the distribution of the sale proceeds.

A live-together-until-we-get-into-a-giant-fight agreement would contain most of the same matters, except that the responsibility for paying carrying costs is usually shared. Often the formula for distribution of sale proceeds takes into account uneven contributions to the carrying costs and improvements.

111

Regardless of how unusual the arrangement may be, nothing prevents a tenancy in common agreement from being drafted to suit the parties' needs. A sample parent-child agreement is set forth in Appendix H to give an idea of what it might contain. While agents should be informed about what an "equity share" or, as it is more properly called, a "tenancy in common agreement" entails, remember that drafting such an agreement goes far beyond the permissible activities of a real estate licensee. Because the agreement involves more than just filling out a routine contract, and requires knowledge of several areas of the law, including tax regulations, it is mandatory that you refer clients to competent legal counsel for further explanation and the actual drafting of the document. And remember, a personal injury lawyer probably knows less about a tenancy in common agreement than you do. Advise your clients to obtain advice from an attorney specializing in real estate transactions.

Attorneys in some areas, also licensed as real estate brokers, do nothing but draft tenancy in common agreements. As noted below, these attorneys usually promote equity-sharing as a selling tool, and the agreements they use are often not suited to family or live-together transactions.

2. Investor Sharing

Young couples are particularly prone to equity sharing arrangements with third-party investors. Maybe Mom and Dad just do not have the money to help out with the down payment or, as is often the case, the kids want to show their parents they can get along on their own. In slow markets the seller often acts as the third-party investor, agreeing to participate by contributing what would otherwise be a twenty percent down payment to the tenancy in common. The seller-investor then puts the burden of carrying the property on the buyers, receives some cash from the refinancing, and can expect to recoup the down-payment investment on the eventual resale, together with a share of any appreciation in value.

Actually, the buyers, sometimes referred to as the "Resident Owners," are least likely to suffer financially in such transactions. If they cannot maintain the monthly payments, then they can walk away and leave the "Investor Owner" to salvage the transaction. No one has yet devised a method for the investor to quickly obtain title to the property and still hold the resident owners personally liable for any damages the investor suffers. Generally, anti-deficiency laws in California protect the buyers from personal liability.[132] These laws limit a lender's recourse to the property and do not permit a personal deficiency judgment against the borrower. The flip side of the coin is that the buyers' credit, to say nothing of their self-esteem, can be shredded if they fail to make payments. Hardly a good way to start out their adult lives.

If things go sour, the investor has the most serious problem. Normally, the investor's remedy would be for breach of contract, a suit for partition, a quiet title action, or a combination of these. These are time consuming and expensive. In addition, pending resolution of the litigation, the investor must make monthly payments on any encumbrances to make certain defaults are not filed, as well as keep up any other expenses of the property.

Some lawyers and brokers lay awake long hours trying to figure out how the equity investor can quickly regain title where the occupier flakes out. Supposedly legal solutions are sometimes incorporated in a form called an "Equity Sharing Agreement."

---

[132]Calif. Code of Civil Procedure §§580a, 580b and 580d.

So far these agreements have not been recognized by authoritative court decisions as being legally acceptable.

One solution makes the buyer a tenant under a lease agreement as well as a tenant in common. The agreement usually provides that in the event of default, the investor-owner can evict the resident-owner with an unlawful detainer action, which is a summary proceeding. But each co-tenant enjoys the right of possession to the entire property absent an agreement to the contrary. While a breach of the agreement to pay rent might be sufficient to oust the resident-owner as a lessee, there is considerable doubt whether it is sufficient to remove him from possession as a tenant in common.[133]

The "Equity Sharing Agreement" entitles the investor to take a portion of the depreciation on the property but he or she must report rental payment as income. Tax benefits from interest payments on the loans are shared by both participants under a formula set forth in the agreement. The investor, as well as being a lessor, also has the benefit of an all-inclusive note and deed of trust to secure the performance by the owner-occupier. One would think that this approach makes the investor a "lender," thereby jeopardizing his or her equity investor status.

113

Again, the question arises whether such a deed of trust is valid. Under the doctrine of "merger," an owner of real property cannot secure a valid lien on it in his or her own favor.[134] It seems, therefore, that the lien of the deed of trust would merge with the interest of the investor (since the investor is both a beneficiary of the deed of trust and owner of an undivided interest in the property on which the deed of trust purports to create a lien).

These various devices to protect the investor may also run afoul of recent rulings that co-tenants stand in a fiduciary relationship to each other. This precludes one co-tenant from asserting an adverse claim or title without the knowing consent of the other co-tenant.[135]

---

[133]Proponents of such plans try to avoid the problem by having the "occupier" sign a lease for the portion of the property he "does not own." However, since a tenant in common owns an undivided interest in "all" of the property, the legitimacy of this device is highly questionable.

[134]See *Lee v. Joseph* (1968) 267 Cal.App. 30, 35; 72 Cal.Rptr. 471.

[135]*Wilson v. S. L. Rey, Inc.* (1993) 17 Cal.App.4th 234; 21 Cal.Rptr.2d 552.

114

If this seems terribly complicated, you can imagine the difficulty in explaining the proposed transaction to an unsophisticated buyer or investor. In her book *"The Complete Guide to Equity Sharing,"*[136] the author, Marilyn Sullivan, appropriately acknowledges that "The equity share transaction is technical and complex. It presents a challenge for even the most skilled practitioner." I concur. **Only attorneys should draft the required agreement and supporting documents**. Their clients should also satisfy themselves that their counsel carries ample malpractice insurance coverage. They will need it.

The inherent complexity of investor-type equity share agreement prompts some enterprising agents to market a far simpler scheme. It uses a quitclaim deed assuring the investor can obtain title in the event of default by the occupying co-tenant. The investor puts up the down payment, usually 10 percent of the purchase price. The occupier qualifies for the loan, carries all of the monthly service costs (including the mortgage, insurance and taxes), and receives the deductions. After five years, the property must be sold (or purchased by the occupier for fair market value). From the proceeds the loan is paid, the investor receives the down payment, and the equity is split equally between the investor and the occupier.

To make certain the occupier keeps all of the carrying costs current, the investor receives a quitclaim deed to the property which he can record upon any default by the occupier. The occupier must send the investor copies of the monthly mortgage statement or cancelled checks as proof that payments remain current.

Obvious flaws mar such transactions. The occupier could probably challenge the quitclaim deed on the ground that it is a subterfuge for a security interest. The investor could record the quitclaim deed without a default or where a default is in dispute. Neither party enjoys much protection.

In any event, why would any investor be interested in such a deal unless expecting astronomical appreciation in real property values? The answer is that more often than not the broker is the investor, a fact often not revealed to the occupier. For the broker, this can be a no-lose situation. The broker will receive a six percent commission from the original seller. The broker gets an additional three percent under a deal with the

---

[136](1992) Venture 2000 Publishers, P.O. Box 625, Larkspur, CA 94977-0625 (Tel: 1-800-843-6701).

parties whereby the purchase price is inflated for "non-recurring closing costs" which sum finds its way into the broker's pocket. All the broker has to do is come up with another one percent of the purchase price to satisfy the down payment requirements, and it has just become a 50 percent owner of a residential property. As a sweetener, the tenancy in common agreement provides that when the property is resold at the end of the five-year period, it must be listed with the broker or the broker receives, in lieu of the listing, seven percent of the market value of the property from the co-tenants (which is really three and one-half percent since the broker is one of the co-tenants).

The offenses being committed by the broker include practicing law without a license; failing to reveal secret profits to a fiduciary; defrauding institutional lenders; various federal tax violations; obtaining a listing without a termination date; and conspiracy to defraud both the buyer and the seller of the real property involved. When these offenses were called to the attention of one large brokerage firm by an attorney reviewing the firm's in-house prepared documentation, the broker accused the attorney of trying to kill the deal, claiming the practice was so common place that it was stupid to allege wrongdoing. Moreover, the broker refused to let the attorney make any copies of any of the documentation because it constituted a "trade secret." Presumably that broker will wind up in jail or at least will be missing a license.

115

Under present laws, equity sharing arrangements as a selling tool do not ordinarily work. In some commercial transactions, and where relatives or significant others are involved, the device can be very useful. It must be drafted by real estate counsel with experience in the field. Under no circumstances should the agent attempt to produce, or even negotiate, the mechanics of such transactions.

D. Non-recurring Closing Costs

Whenever I see the phrase **"non-recurring closing costs"** in an escrow document, I know that a crime may be in progress. The purchase price is probably being inflated to obtain a higher loan, with the kickback going to the buyer (or sometimes the broker). Agents tell me that their loan brokers advise them that "non-recurring closing costs" which do not exceed three percent of the purchase price are permissible. Check this out with the bank examiners or the secondary mortgage market, such as

Fannie Mae or Freddie Mac. They will tell you that **any** false inflation of the purchase price is illegal and will be prosecuted. Even seizure of the residence from the buyer is authorized under recent case law.

Parties to a purchase agreement can certainly negotiate who is going to pay the closing costs. For example, the escrow instructions can provide that the seller will pay the title insurance out of the sale proceeds, an expense ordinarily paid by the buyer in many areas. The parties can also negotiate as to who will pay the mortgage loan fee, real estate commission, escrow fees, the one-year home warranty fee, or the transfer fees. This is significantly different from simply adding $5,000 or $10,000 to the purchase price and then crediting this amount to the buyer in escrow.

In one case involving "non-recurring closing costs" the plaintiff obtained a $590,000 settlement shortly before trial. The facts of the case would impress even a sophisticated swindler. According to the pleadings, Frank, a popular real estate agent associated with a broker of impeccable reputation, gained the confidence of Delores, a client with cash. He persuaded her to join forces with his live-in-companion, Jim, to acquire real estate for investment purposes. In a typical transaction involving a four-unit building, Frank asked the sellers to increase the purchase price by $44,000 in order to obtain a larger loan and provide deferred maintenance with the extra proceeds.

The listing agent agreed that her commission would be based on the original price. The sellers, not suffering any difference in the net sale proceeds, saw no problem in increasing the contract price. A loan application was submitted to the loan broker based on the increased value. With a little massaging of the income figures, an acceptable appraisal was obtained. The loan broker conveniently forgot that the investor had just purchased another residence for herself and could not physically be an "owner-occupier" of one of the units to be acquired as she indicated on the loan application.

Frank and Jim asked the title company to prepare escrow instructions for the seller whereby the title company would disburse the $44,000 as a non-recurring closing cost to a "D. Jones," the contractor who supposedly would do the work. D. Jones turned out to be another agent in the same office who, believing she was only acting as a conduit in a friendly transaction, picked up the check from the title company in the company of the selling agent and went to the bank to deposit it in Jim's account.

The transaction was reviewed by Frank's broker, as required by the real estate regulations. Neither the broker, the seller's agent, the title company, or the sellers ever asked about "D. Jones," and no repair work was ever done. Frank not only received his share of the commission, but he and Jim spent the $44,000.

The pleadings allege that Frank and Jim's swindling of Delores, admittedly not a very astute business person, was repeated on several other occasions involving the same loan broker and title company. Delores eventually wound up in bankruptcy, and Frank and Jim died of AIDS. Although the case was settled before trial, the evidence of the scheme was persuasive. Frank's broker, the loan broker, Jim's estate (Frank's estate was insolvent) and, to a modest degree, the other agents in the transactions, participated in the settlement. Remember that in a real estate transaction the broker is liable for the conduct of the agents acting under its license even if that conduct involves intentional fraud.

While this case is unusual in the scope of the alleged fraud, the same potential exists in every "non-recurring closing cost" situation. Do not be a party, even passively, to this kind of scheme. The fact that a loan broker may condone it or look the other way, or that "all the other agents are doing it," does not make it legal or justifiable.

117

Some brokers have recently been using "non-recurring closing costs" to fund equity-sharing arrangements (which is described as a "Real Estate Investment Partnership"). The "investor" turns out to be the broker who, with the commission and non-recurring closing costs, can become a 50% tenant in common without any investment at all. The owner-occupiers never figure out that their monthly payments on the mortgage are also paying back the "non-recurring closing costs."[137]

Always approach "non-recurring closing costs" with suspicion.

[137]For a more detailed discussion of equity-sharing arrangements as a selling tool, see pages 110 *et seq.*

118

Part VII
Alternative Dispute Resolution

Since July 1, 1992 all California courts must implement the "**Fast Track**" program. In addition, many counties have adopted the Alternative Dispute Resolution (ADR) program. Lawyers generally admire the goals justifying these programs, but complain vociferously about the difficulties they pose to legal practice and the possible loss of constitutional safeguards. Every real estate agent and broker needs a working knowledge of these programs. This is particularly helpful when a prospective seller or buyer asks about arbitration and mediation clauses in the purchase agreement. ADR and "fast track" substantially influence whether these clauses should be initialed by the parties. Knowing about them is essential for educating your clients about their options. Making specific recommendations, however, should be avoided. Once they understand these options, a decision should be left strictly to the parties to the agreement.

119

A. The Impact of "Fast Track"

"Fast track" has been used experimentally in some counties for several years. Here is how it works. When a complaint is filed, the plaintiff receives a notice of the case's assignment to a particular judge. As in federal courts, this judge handles the case until it is tried. He hears all motions and resolves any pre-trial disputes. This judge is also responsible for seeing that the case moves forward to trial **no later than one year** from the filing date. This means depositions, interrogatories, inspections, and all discovery must be handled in a timely fashion. Rules state that 90% of the cases must be disposed of within 12 months. With special dispensation, 8% are to be disposed of in 18 months, with the remaining 2% no later than 24 months.

To maintain this rigorous schedule, the judge sets frequent "status" conferences. All the attorneys **and their clients** are usually required to attend. Failure to attend or to be prepared to solve the problem at hand leads to monetary sanctions imposed by the court. The cash register jingles each morning the court is in session.

B. The Pros and Cons of "ADR"

ADR kicks in at the first status conference. The court gives the parties the option of deciding whether they want mediation, judicial arbitration, non-binding private arbitration, or binding arbitration. Since parties to a real estate contract commonly ask about these various forms of ADR, agents should be prepared to give a basic explanation, particularly since mediation and binding arbitration are choices offered in most purchase agreements.

1. Judicial Arbitration

Judicial arbitration is a program many California courts adopt when cases fall below a certain dollar amount, usually $50,000. The term "judicial arbitration" has been criticized since the system is not judicial in nature nor the arbitration binding. The court maintains a list of attorneys who volunteer to act as arbitrators (at a modest fee, usually $150 per day) and randomly selects a panel which is submitted to the parties. Each party is allowed one challenge. The arbitrator is selected from the remaining names on the list — often just one person. The arbitrator holds a hearing, taking evidence under rules usually much more informal than in a court proceeding. He or she issues a decision which, though not binding on the parties, often results in settlement since it indicates how the case might be decided if it went to trial. If the parties do reach a settlement, it must be in writing or approved in open court. Approval by the arbitrator is not sufficient.

If the case is not settled, either party can request a trial *de novo* (a "new trial"). Some relatively minor penalties are assessed against a party if, at the trial *de novo,* that party fails to achieve a result more favorable than that rendered by the arbitrator.

Judicial arbitration is out of favor in some courts because the time given under the rules to conduct the arbitration and ask for trial *de novo* conflicts with the speed required from "fast track" time tables. In addition, the court, not the parties, pays for judicial arbitration. However, the court frequently orders the parties to go to judicial arbitration, particularly if they waive the time constraints.

2. Mediation

Mediation does not involve a decision by a third party. Instead, the arbitrator helps the parties resolve the conflict by mutual agreement. Many mediators can skillfully facilitate negotiations, pointing out weaknesses in the arguments and suggesting ways to settle the dispute which may not have occurred to either party. Special courses train mediators in this work and they often can create a climate free from acrimony.

120

Some mediators follow up on the telephone with the parties or their attorneys and, on reaching agreement, help prepare the memorandum settling the matter.

3. Non-binding Private Arbitration

Non-binding private arbitration is like judicial arbitration except that the parties select the arbitrator and pay the arbitrator's fees. It is currently favored in "fast track" proceedings because the court can order that it be completed in a relatively short period of time. If the parties have difficulty selecting an arbitrator, the court will do it for them.

4. Binding Arbitration

Binding arbitration usually occurs when a disputed contract provides for arbitration. In agreements of sale, such provisions must be printed in a certain size of type, explain the effects of arbitration, and be initialed by the parties "to indicate their assent or nonassent to the arbitration provision."[138] Some forms of purchase agreement do not give the parties the option to indicate their nonassent,[139] implying that there is no other alternative. **Without a place to initial nonassent, the form itself cannot be referred to as evidence that you, the agent, explained the options which your client could evaluate and choose.** If arbitration is declined, note this fact on the form, writing "declined."

RECOMMEND

121

Moreover, a recent case held that where one party initials the arbitration clause but the other does not, the party that does not initial can still compel the initialling party to arbitration, even though the non-initialing party cannot be compelled to arbitrate.[140] The court distinguished the liquidated damage provision, which it acknowledged requires the initials of both parties to be valid.[141] If the issue arises, this distinction will be difficult to explain to the parties except to say that appellate courts sometimes engage in technical mischief.

In any event, it seems fairer if both or neither of the parties are compelled to arbitrate. Mutuality of remedy, which certainly appears fairer to the layman, would probably occur if the

---

[138]Calif. Code of Civil Procedure §1298 (c).

[139]The CAR and Coldwell Banker forms only provide a space for assent.

[140]*Grubb & Ellis Company v. Bello* (1993) 19 Cal.App.4th 231; 23 Cal.Rptr.2d 281.

[141]The court relied upon the language of Calif. Civil Code §1677 which provides that the liquidated damage provision is invalid unless "[t]he provision is separately signed or initialed by each party to the contract. . . ."

contract form used provides places for the parties to initial both assent and dissent to arbitration. Then, if one party assents and the other dissents, it could be asserted that a counter offer has in fact been made and the desires of the parties in this regard can be harmonized.[142]

Arbitration clauses provide for a variety of rules governing proceedings. The procedures must be reasonable, however, or the arbitration provision may be unenforceable. For example, a provision in a California contract providing that any dispute will be resolved by binding arbitration by the National Arbitration Forum in Minneapolis, Minnesota, was held, under the circumstances, to be unconscionable and unenforceable.[143]

As ADR becomes more familiar, parties are using innovative procedures. One popular method is the "high-low" format. The parties agree on a maximum and minimum recovery. If the arbitrator's award is somewhere between the high-low, that decision is binding. If the amount of the award is above or below the high-low, then the high or low figure becomes the award.

Many arbitration clauses incorporate either the rules of the American Arbitration Association, which provides a roster of qualified arbitrators, or the provisions of the California Arbitration Act set forth in sections 1280 *et seq.* of the California Code of Civil Procedure.[144] Under either approach, the formal rules of evidence do not apply and pre-arbitration discovery is limited. The hearing is conducted by an arbitrator selected by the parties, or by petition to the court if the parties cannot agree.

The American Arbitration Association is a non-profit organization that has been in business since 1926. It has a roster of arbitrators. They may be accountants, lawyers, real estate brokers, or others, experienced in the field in which the dispute has arisen. The arbitrator is often a retired judge associated with JAMS (Judicial Arbitration and Mediation Services) or ENDISP-

122

---

[142]The *Bello* case, cited in footnote 140, *supra*, calls into question whether, even if a party indicates that they "do not agree" to arbitration, they can nevertheless invoke arbitration against the party who has initialled the "agree" provision in the arbitration clause.

[143]*Patterson v. ITT Consumer Financial Corp.* (1993) 14 Cal.App.4th 1659; 18 Cal.Rptr.2d 563.

[144]For undisclosed reasons, the CAR form of purchase agreement gives parties the choice between the rules of the American Arbitration Association or the Judicial Arbitration and Mediation Services (JAMS).

UTE. JAMS is the largest for-profit arbitration firm and has revenues in excess of $30 million per year. However, ENDISPU-TE is rapidly growing and is favored by many lawyers.

Stockbrokers, health organizations and recently banks and other businesses have begun inserting arbitration clauses in their contracts as a condition of doing business with them. Critics of forced arbitration claim that in time the arbitrators become prejudiced in favor of business and do not give an individual claimant a fair shake. Whether this criticism is valid as applied to the real estate industry remains to be seen, although since most of the disputes are between individual buyers and sellers there would seem to be little reason for strong leanings by the arbitrator one way or the other. Arbitration undoubtedly is favored by brokers and their errors and omissions insurance carriers since it keeps misconduct issues away from juries inclined to large awards. This may be the reason that the arbitration clause in the CAR form does not give the buyer or seller the option to indicate that they decline, other than by failing to initial the paragraph. However, arbitration often is not the appropriate remedy for the buyer or seller, and, as fiduciaries, an agent is obligated to look out for clients before they attempt to limit their own liability.

In many states the award of the arbitrator is not enforceable. However, in California the award can be affirmed by a court as a judgment and enforced as a judgment.[145]

The arbitrator's decision cannot be challenged except where the arbitrator exceeds his or her authority. There is no recourse for mistakes by the arbitrator in applying the law or in interpreting the facts.[146] The arbitrator enjoys the same immunity as a judge from civil liability when acting as an arbitrator.[147] Neither the arbitrator nor the sponsoring organization (for example, the American Arbitration Association), can be held liable for negligence or breach of contract.[148]

While contracts can provide that the arbitrator's decision is subject to appeal, such provisions are rare. In other words, by

123

---

[145]Calif. Code of Civil Procedure §1287.4.

[146]*Hall v. Superior Court (Trompas)* (1993) 18 Cal.App.4th 427; 22 Cal.Rptr.2d 376.

[147]Calif. Code of Civil Procedure §1280.1.

[148]*Thiele v. RML Realty Partners* (1993) 14 Cal.App.4th 1526; 18 Cal.Rptr.-2d 416.

selecting binding arbitration your client essentially gives up his or her right to a jury trial, guaranteed by the Seventh Amendment to the Constitution, and the right to appeal. A binding arbitration award will not be overturned even if, on its face, it is contrary to established rules of law.[149] However, the court in a recent case noted that the policy favoring finality of arbitration decisions does not protect an error so egregious that the result is completely outside the expectations of the parties to the contract.[150]

While it cannot be disputed that arbitration saves substantial money and results in a prompt determination, the idea that an arbitrator with no judicial experience can hold your fate in his hands is sobering. Too frequently I have experienced arbitrators who, having a "bad day," issued disturbingly erroneous decisions. Many law firms and sole practitioners are giving up their practices to do nothing but mediation and arbitration. Obviously, they sense the enormous profits to be made with ADR. Many lawyers are more comfortable with retired judges from JAMS or ENDISPUTE acting as arbitrators or mediators, even though they can be expensive.

An example of one result that can be reached is demonstrated by a controversy involving a buy-sell agreement for a residence with a $600,000 purchase price. The buyer put down $21,000, making the purchase subject to obtaining conventional financing. During inspections, the buyer discovered the foundation needed repair work, which he planned to address over a period of time. The lender, however, insisted that money be set aside from the purchase loan to do the repair. The buyer got a bid of $30,000, and realized that setting aside this amount meant not having enough cash to close. He notified the seller that he could not meet the loan contingency and the offer expired. The seller, however, got a bid of $6,000 for the repair, which was satisfactory to the lender, and offered to do the fix himself so the buyer could close. Now the buyer, however, decided he did not want to go ahead and claimed that since they were out of contract, he should get his deposit back. The seller thought differently, claiming that since the buyer knew about the foundation problem, he did not use good faith in trying to satisfy the loan contingency, particularly in light of the

---

[149]*Moncharsh v. Heily & Blaise* (1992) 3 Cal.4th 1; 10 Cal.Rptr.2d 183.

[150]*Pacific Gas and Elec. Co. v. Superior Court (Ansacapa Oil Corp.)* (1993) 15 Cal.App.4th 576; 19 Cal.Rptr.2d 295.

seller's offer to do the repair. When the seller subsequently sold the house for $575,000, he claimed the full $21,000 down payment from the first offer as damages.

The contract had a binding arbitration clause which the parties exercised. They both retained counsel, and written briefs were presented to the arbitrator, selected from a panel submitted by the American Arbitration Association. The arbitrator was an experienced and recognized real estate broker in the community. He held a hearing, took testimony from witnesses, and carefully reviewed the briefs submitted by the attorneys.

Legally, this was an all or nothing deal. Either the buyer or the seller was entitled to the full $21,000, plus attorney fees and costs. The arbitrator, however, awarded $5,000 to the seller, $16,000 to the buyer, and concluded that since neither party was the prevailing party, they would each bear their own costs and attorney fees.

By the time the parties had concluded the arbitration process, they had each spent about $2,800 in attorney fees. If they had litigated the matter, attorney fees and costs for each undoubtedly would have exceeded $20,000. The arbitration process clearly saved the parties money and kept the controversy out of the court system.

125

Was justice accomplished? The arbitrator certainly did not follow the law — he made an award he thought was fair without regard to legal niceties. The parties had no right to challenge his decision. However, while both were unhappy with the decision, they also felt grateful for the opportunity to tell their stories. Here ADR seemed to work, even though the result was unpredictable.

Although authorized, arbitrators rarely, if ever, award punitive damages. Occasionally the conduct of a party or an agent is so egregious that such damages are appropriate. Or, as is often the case, liability rests solely on the credibility of a witness, who may be the buyer, the seller, or one of the agents. The jury system was designed specifically for this purpose, and the decision a jury reaches with regard to the believability of witnesses, though more expensive and time-consuming, is unquestionably more reliable and fair than that of an arbitrator. Relinquishing the right of appeal should not be lightly undertaken.

For these and similar reasons, the growing consensus is that the buyer and seller are best served if they do not initial the arbitration clause but wait to see whether the amount and nature of the controversy makes it suitable for arbitration. If it is, they can mutually decide to use binding arbitration if and when a dispute arises.

C. Explain — Do Not Recommend!

126

Court ordered ADR will usually not be involved where the parties have already agreed in the purchase agreement to invoke mediation, arbitration, or both. If one party fails to cooperate, a petition can be filed with the Superior Court for the appointment of an arbitrator. While mediation can be required by the court before any litigation goes forward, neither you nor your clients can be forced to submit to binding arbitration unless you agree. The Constitution guarantees the right to a jury trial and the right of appeal.[151]

When you explain the various options that your clients have regarding alternative dispute resolution, the mediation option is the least significant since the court usually requires mediation *in appropriate cases* at a very early stage in the litigation if the parties have not already chosen to utilize it.[152] Insisting on mediation in the contract could have serious consequences. For example, the current CAR purchase contract form (DLF-14, Revised 8/93) provides that when an action is filed without first using mediation, that party waives the contractual right to recover attorney's fees.[153] Taking away the parties rights to determine for themselves whether to incur the time and expense for mediation — which may not even be appropriate for their particular dispute — appears presumptuous. Often it is necessary to immediately file litigation to avoid the bar of the statute of

---

[151] See *Bayscene Resident v. Bayscene Mobilehome* (1993) 15 Cal.App.4th 119; 18 Cal.Rptr.2d 626.

[152] Florida and Texas require mediation before litigating a dispute.

[153] The form curiously provides that the effectiveness of the waiver then rests in the discretion of the arbitrator or judge. Since such discretion already exists, the interpretation of this clause will have to await judicial review.

limitations. The impact of this clause on such action is unclear. For example, if a buyer discovers, 23 months after close of escrow, that the seller failed to properly fill out the TDS, the buyer only has one month to file suit before his cause of action is barred by Civil Code §2079.4. If the buyer must go through mediation first, he or she will lose the right to sue.

Recent legislation requires that, before a suit is filed between a condominium owner and the homeowner's association seeking declaratory or injunctive relief under the CC&Rs, the parties must submit to binding or nonbinding alternative dispute resolution. The requirement is waived, however, where the statute of limitations would run in 120 days, or where more than $5,000 in damages is involved. The CAR requirement does not have such safeguards.

RECOMMEND

Mediation can be comparatively expensive. The American Arbitration Association has a $300 filing fee and the mediator charges $200 per hour. Other mediation services with less name recognition advertise rates as low as $100 per hour per party. Local governmental agencies also sponsor less expensive mediation services. Using a retired judge from JAMS or ENDISPUTE raises the cost considerably. In a typical four-party dispute (buyer, seller, listing agent, and selling agent) JAMS charges are $500 per hour. ENDISPUTE currently charges $1,300 per half day and $2,400 for a full day.

127

Some disputes simply do not warrant this cost. Mediation can always be elected by the parties if it is not required by the court. The mediation clause should be stricken unless both parities clearly understand and concur in its inclusion.

As indicated above, most informed parties, and particularly buyers, elect not to initial the arbitration clause. Having invested so much in the purchase, they conclude that giving up their constitutional rights is not worth the possible savings in time and money — particularly when there is no remedy for a completely unjustified result.

CAUTION

The agent's job is to explain the meaning of alternative dispute resolution choices given in the contract of sale. The agent should not make recommendations. If, for example, the agent makes a recommendation that the arbitration clause be initialed, and the client later discovers that he or she has no recourse from a completely arbitrary and unfavorable decision, you can be certain that the client will look to the agent for satisfaction of some sort. Let your client make the decision. Be certain, however, that the client has been advised of the options available. Failure to do so is conduct below the Standard of Care.

128

Conclusion

Most brokerage firms budget litigation costs and treat lawsuits as routine business episodes. The ordinary agent is not so experienced. It is difficult to describe the emotional reaction that agents suffer when they are threatened with litigation or actually served with a complaint. Anxiety and despair are common reactions. A frequent question asked by prospective agents in educational courses on risk management is, "Why do I want to go into a profession that has this kind of exposure and hassle?"

It is true that persons entering the real estate industry should be aware that they are expected to perform carefully and to exercise their fiduciary duties toward their clients in an honest and competent manner. Those who specialize in defending real estate agents are uniform in their criticism that the public and the courts hold agents to unrealistically high standards.

Nevertheless, the rewards, both financial and professional, can be substantial. To avoid the risk of litigation, the agent must be constantly vigilant of situations that commonly lead to allegations of misrepresentation and negligence. Experience has shown that these factual situations are repetitive and relatively few in number. Attending seminars on updates of current court decisions, changes in forms and contracts, and other risk management courses is vital.

It is also essential that the agent be protected by adequate errors and omissions coverage, whether from an institutional carrier or a self-insurance program provided by the broker.

With this protection and awareness, the agent who documents all significant activities in a transaction (e.g., telephone calls and property visits) will find that the probability of being sued is greatly reduced.

Obtaining adequate insurance and acting within the Standard of Care are the key elements of risk management for the agent. Brokers must always keep in mind that they are vicariously responsible for the conduct of their agents, even if that conduct consists of intentional fraud of which the broker is completely unaware. Careful recruiting, follow-up supervision, and ongoing educational programs for the agent are the broker's risk management duties.

For both the broker and the agent, practicing reasonable risk management will lead to a successful and litigation-free real estate careers.

Take Care,
Jim McKenney

Appendices

131

132

NOTICE REGARDING SEPTIC SYSTEMS

(This is a disclosure form in addition to the required statutory transfer disclosure statement. It is not a warranty and is not intended to be a part of the contract between the Buyer and Seller.)

PROPERTY:_____

1. The above-identified Property is not presently connected to a public sewer system. Waste water disposal is by a private individual septic system located on the property. If a public system is developed in the future, the property owner may be required to connect to such system at the owner's cost.

2. The design, quality, and condition of individual septic systems can vary widely, and individual systems can be in good condition or can be virtually nonexistent and completely failing. A septic system is an underground structure that cannot be easily inspected and may be difficult to locate on the Property, even by experts. In fact, complete inspection of a system could be destructive to the system itself. Besides the system's design and physical condition, the performance of a septic system also can vary strongly with seasons, soil conditions, slope, water table characteristics, load, and physical use of the property. Past and present performance of the system is not necessarily a predictor of future performance, and systems can "wear out" over time. A septic system can have many problems that cannot be easily determined even by a person skilled in inspecting septic systems. Problems can include failure to meet code requirements, insufficient capacity, inadequate or failing leach lines, inadequate or defective tanks, undersize tanks, infiltration by roots, crushed or separated pipe, and damage from improper use and maintenance. An improperly functioning system can be expensive to correct, can be a major nuisance, and can even cause serious health problems. In rare cases, the impossibility of constructing any acceptable system on a property can result in abatement of the use of the property for dwelling purposes.

133

3. Expansion (for example, in case of any remodeling of the dwelling or to replace failed septic systems), maintenance, repair, and replacement of septic systems can be expensive and, under some circumstances, may not be permitted under current codes, requiring the adoption of more expensive alternative to the existing system. Additionally, expansion may be conditioned on conducting a successful percolation test on the property, which generally can only be done during certain times of the year and depends on weather conditions and ground water levels. Many existing septic systems were built prior to the adoption of the current codes and do not comply with current codes. Additionally, applicable codes can and do change, and systems meeting current codes may not meet future requirements. Permits are generally required for all maintenance and repair work done on a system, other than routine pumping.

4. **THE REAL ESTATE AGENTS ARE NOT EXPERTS REGARDING SEPTIC SYSTEMS AND HAVE NO SPECIAL KNOWLEDGE OR ABILITY CONCERNING SEPTIC SYSTEMS AND INSPECTION OF SEPTIC SYSTEMS.** The Seller has not disclosed to Seller's Agent or Buyer's Agent any problems with the septic system except those listed in the Real Estate Transfer Disclosure Statement. Buyer's Agent and Seller's Agent have conducted a visual inspection of the Property (within the limits required of them under California law as real estate licensees) for indications of problems with the system and have not discovered any such indications except those that are listed in the Transfer Disclosure Statement. Among the most frequent signs of possible problems with a septic system that may be observed in such a nonexpert inspection are odor and sewage on or dampness of the surface of the property. Other indications could be back-up of water in the tank and back-up of waste lines in the house. All of these conditions can be irregular in occurrence and may not be evident on inspection, or could be caused by problems unrelated to the septic system, and the absence of these indications does not mean that there are no problems with the septic system. Also Buyer should be aware that redwood tanks, which are common in the Property's area and could exist on Property, do not meet current code and that

most redwood tanks are at the age that problems with the tanks are likely, and that the code requires replacement of the entire tank if any part of a redwood tank needs repair.

5. The fact that the Buyer's Agent or the Seller's Agent has not discovered any indications concerning potential problems with the septic system does **not** mean that there are no current problems with the septic system or that problems could not develop. **THE AGENTS URGE THE BUYER TO CONDUCT THE BUYER'S OWN INSPECTION OF THE PROPERTY AND TO HAVE THE SEPTIC SYSTEM THOROUGHLY INSPECTED BY LICENSED, COMPETENT PROFESSIONALS SELECTED BY THE BUYER.** (By giving the Buyer the names of inspectors, the Agents do not warrant or guaranty in any way the work of the inspector.) A competent expert inspection should include, among other things, testing for sufficient fluid-handling capacity, an examination of the property, pumping and visually inspecting the tank and, where considered necessary, exposing and inspecting a portion of the leach lines. Visual inspection alone of the tank is usually insufficient. **THE AGENTS DO NOT WARRANT THE CONDITION OF THE SEPTIC SYSTEM AND ARE NOT RESPONSIBLE FOR ANY PROBLEMS WITH THE SYSTEM.**

Buyers acknowledge receipt of a copy of this statement on the date indicated:

Date: _____   _____ Buyer

Date: _____   _____ Buyer

134

"AS IS" ADDENDUM

To Agreement Dated_____ Between_____Seller

And_____ Buyer, Concerning Property Located At

_____.

The property being sold is not new and neither Seller nor Seller's agent warrant the condition of the property, which is to be sold in its present **"AS IS"** condition. This provision shall supersede all other provisions in the Purchase Agreement regarding maintenance, except that Seller agrees that the property (including all structures, pool, spa, grounds and landscaping) will be delivered to Buyer at close of escrow in the same or better condition than as of the time the inspection condition is removed.

Buyer has been advised to carefully inspect the property personally and to obtain inspection reports from qualified experts as to any and all systems and features of the property, including, but not limited to boundary lines, lot and dwelling size, roof, plumbing, electrical, appliances, sewers, septic (where applicable), soil conditions, foundation, heating, air conditioning, structural, and pool and related equipment (where applicable).

Seller agrees to permit Buyer, and Buyer's representatives, reasonable access to the premises for ten (10) business days after acceptance, to complete and approve said inspections.

Unless Buyer notifies Seller within fifteen (15) business days from date of acceptance, in writing, that the condition of the premises is unacceptable (in which event the contract shall become null and void), Buyer agrees to accept the property in its present "as is" condition as of the time the inspection condition is satisfied. Should Buyer find the property unacceptable, the Purchase Agreement shall terminate and be of no further force of effect.

135

Buyer acknowledges that Buyer is not relying upon any representations of the Seller or the Seller's agent as to the condition of the property, the size or boundary lines, nor is Buyer relying upon Seller or Seller's agent to investigate and report on the condition of the property other than conditions known by the Seller and noted on the Transfer Disclosure Statement, and the report on the visual inspection conducted by the agents, also contained in the Transfer Disclosure Statement. In all other respects, Buyer agrees that he or she is relying exclusively upon Buyer's own inspection and that of experts retained by Buyer as to the condition and physical features of the property.

Seller understands that even though this is an "AS IS" sale, the Seller is obligated by law to reveal all known defects of a material nature of which the Seller is aware.

_____   _____
Buyer   Date

_____   _____
Buyer   Date

_____   _____
Seller   Date

_____   _____
Seller   Date

136

"AS IS" ADDENDUM
AND WAIVER OF CIVIL CODE § 1102 ET SEQ.
[TRANSFER DISCLOSURE STATEMENT]

To Agreement Dated_____Between_____Seller

AND_____ Buyer, Concerning Property Located At

_____.

The property being sold is not new and neither Seller nor Seller's agent warrant the condition of the property, which is to be sold in its present **"AS IS"** condition. This provision shall supersede all other provisions in the Purchase Agreement regarding maintenance, and constitutes a waiver of the provisions of Civil Code sections 1102 et seq. requiring that Seller furnish the Buyer with a Transfer Disclosure Statement.

Buyer has been advised to carefully inspect the property personally and to obtain inspection reports from qualified experts as to any and all systems and features of the property, including, but not limited to boundary lines, lot and dwelling size, roof, plumbing, electrical, appliances, sewers, septic (where applicable), soil conditions, foundation, heating, air conditioning, structural, and pool and related equipment (where applicable).

Seller agrees to permit Buyer, and Buyer's representatives, reasonable access to the premises for ten (10) business days after acceptance, to complete and approve said inspections. Unless Buyer notifies Seller within fifteen (15) business days from date of acceptance, in writing, that the condition of the premises is unacceptable (in which event the contract shall become null and void), Buyer agrees to accept the property in its present "as is" and "where is" condition. [The parties understand that this "AS IS" addendum does not relieve the Seller from disclosing material defects of which Seller is aware.]

137

Buyer acknowledges that Buyer is not relying upon any representations of the Seller or the Seller's agent as to the condition of the property, the size or boundary lines, nor is Buyer relying upon Seller or Seller's agent to investigate and report on the condition of the property. Buyer agrees that he or she is relying exclusively upon Buyer's own inspection and that of experts retained by Buyer as to the condition and physical features of the property. Seller agrees that the property will be delivered to Buyer at close of escrow in the same or better condition than as of the time the inspection condition is removed.

_____   _____
Buyer   Date

_____   _____
Buyer   Date

_____   _____
Seller   Date

_____   _____
Seller   Date

138

CONSENT TO DUAL AGENCY

_____ and its agent _____
_____are representing both the
Buyer and the Seller in the sale of real property known as
_____
_____
_____.

     The law specifically recognizes the legality of such dual representation providing that both parties knowingly consent thereto. Since the above-named agent, as a dual agent, owes the duty of undivided loyalty to both parties, there may be situations where a conflict of interest might arise that would preclude the agent from acting fully on behalf of one or the other of the parties. For example, if the agent obtains confidential information from one party, he may not be able to share that information with the other party.

     Notwithstanding this possible conflict, and understanding the further ramifications of the conflict of interest inherent in a dual agency, the undersigned consent to the Broker and Agent acting as agents for both the Buyer and Seller.

Dated: _____   _____

Dated: _____   _____

Dated: _____   _____

Dated: _____   _____

139

140

SAMPLE EXTRACT FROM AN
INDEPENDENT ASSOCIATE AGREEMENT

1.0   OBLIGATIONS OF BROKER

1.1   BROKER agrees to pay all costs and expenses incurred in any dispute or litigation with third parties involving it and INDEPENDENT ASSOCIATE provided such dispute arises out of the normal course of BROKER'S real estate brokerage business. ("The normal course of BROKER'S real estate brokerage business" shall not be deemed to include any situation in which INDEPENDENT ASSOCIATE acts as buyer or seller of real property for his or her own account, directly or indirectly. BROKER shall have no obligation to provide INDEPENDENT ASSOCIATE with a defense against any claim arising out of such a transaction, or for the benefit of or on behalf of any entity in which INDEPENDENT ASSOCIATE may have a direct or indirect interest.) Such costs and expenses shall be defrayed, in part, by the proceeds of a deduction of ____ percent (__%) from all gross commissions payable to BROKER and all of its INDEPENDENT ASSOCIATES, which percentage may be adjusted from time to time with the consent of both parties. [This may also be an annual fee instead of a percentage of commissions.] It is understood that such deduction, hereinafter referred to as the "E & O Fee," shall not be segregated but may be commingled with other funds received by BROKER; provided, however, that records shall be kept to determine whether the deduction [or fee payment] is adequate.

1.2.   BROKER shall defend at its own cost and expense any and all claims made or litigation filed during the term of this agreement, as well as any claims filed after INDEPENDENT ASSOCIATE has terminated his or her relationship with BROKER, provided that the claim arises from any negligent acts or omissions of INDEPENDENT ASSOCIATE in connection with BROKER'S normal real estate brokerage business during the term hereof, as well as satisfy any judgments entered resulting from such negligent acts or omissions.

1.3.   BROKER shall control and shall have the full and exclusive right to prosecute, defend, compromise or settle any disputes or litigation referred to herein above, or otherwise involving the normal course of the BROKER'S business (including suits for commissions) without the agreement or consent of INDEPENDENT ASSOCIATE, providing that any settlement not consented to shall not put the INDEPENDENT ASSOCIATE'S license in jeopardy.

1.4.   INDEPENDENT ASSOCIATE agrees that he or she shall at any time required, whether at that time associated with BROKER, cooperate with the prosecution, defense, compromise or settlement of any disputes or litigation, including but not restricted to participation as a witness for depositions or trial, answering interrogatories or assisting in providing information to the attorneys for BROKER at no further expense to BROKER.

1.5.   Notwithstanding any of the foregoing, it is understood and agreed that broker shall not be responsible for any intentional torts or fraudulent acts of INDEPENDENT ASSOCIATE, it being the intent of these paragraphs 1.0 to provide only for negligent acts and omissions of INDEPENDENT ASSOCIATE. In the event of any intentional tort or fraudulent act by INDEPENDENT ASSOCIATE, the foregoing undertaking and indemnification by BROKER shall be of no force and effect, and INDEPENDENT ASSOCIATE shall be obligated to pay all costs and expenses of any dispute or litigation, as well as any judgment resulting from any intentional tort or fraudulent act not constituting simple negligence by act or omission of INDEPENDENT ASSOCIATE.

1.6.   It is understood that in most cases where a claim or complaint is filed against the BROKER and the INDEPENDENT ASSOCIATE, there are combined allegations sounding both in negligence and in intentional tort or fraud. Under such circumstances, the BROKER will provide counsel to defend INDEPENDENT ASSOCIATE, it being understood, however, that if any judgment rendered is for fraud, or other intentional tort, or for punitive or exemplary damages, said portion of the judgment shall be the sole responsibility of INDEPENDENT ASSOCIATE. Because of the reservation of rights set forth in this paragraph and in paragraph 1.5, a possible conflict of interest could occur between BROKER and INDEPENDENT ASSOCIATE in the event that punitive or exemplary damages are an issue, or where fraud or intentional tort is alleged. (For example, if the INDEPENDENT ASSOCIATE is accused of fraud, BROKER may wish to deny that it participated in or ratified the alleged fraudulent conduct.) It is understood and agreed that, in such an event, INDEPENDENT ASSOCIATE may retain counsel of his or her own choosing to monitor or participate in the litigation, but the cost of said independent counsel shall be borne solely by INDEPENDENT ASSOCIATE. In the event that there is a conflict of interest as provided in Civil Code section 2860, then BROKER shall be responsible for paying the fees of independent counsel as limited in said statute.

1.7.   In the event parties to a transaction in which a commission has been paid voluntarily rescind the transaction, or a judgment of rescission is entered by as court of competent jurisdiction, both BROKER and INDEPENDENT ASSOCIATE shall return their respective portions of the commission if necessary to effectuate the rescission.

1.8.   BROKER shall use it best efforts to provide errors and omissions insurance coverage for itself as well as INDEPENDENT ASSOCIATE. It is understood, however, that the deductible for said insurance is becoming increasingly larger, and the premiums for said insurance may render it economically unfeasible to obtain,. BROKER shall be under no obligation to provide errors and omissions insurance if, by reasonable economic standards for the industry, that insurance coverage is not economically feasible. Failure to provide such insurance, however, shall not relieve BROKER of its obligations under these paragraphs.

ILLUSTRATIVE TENANCY IN COMMON AGREEMENT

RECORDING REQUESTED BY:	
WHEN RECORDED MAIL TO:	

ABOVE SPACE FOR RECORDER'S AND CLERK'S USE

AGREEMENT BETWEEN TENANTS IN COMMON

This Agreement made this 1st day of March 1994, in Sonoma County, California, by and between **JOHN W. SMITH** and **MARY A. SMITH**, his wife, (hereinafter "SMITH"), and **RICHARD FATHER** (hereinafter "FATHER," is made with reference to the following facts:

A. The parties have purchased as co-owners and as tenants in common that certain real property generally known as 1625 Happy Avenue, Sonoma, California 94970 (A.P. #83-063-13), legally described as:

"Lot 3, Block 'M', Sonoma Park Subdivision No. I, as shown upon that certain map thereof filed in Book 'D' of Maps, at page 17, Sonoma County Records."

B. The parties own said property in equal, undivided interests, the undivided 1/2 interest of SMITH being held as community property, and the undivided 1/2 interest of FATHER being held as his sole and separate property.

143

F. The parties desire to enter into the following agreement with respect to the ownership and operation of said property.

THEREFORE, IT IS AGREED AS FOLLOWS:

1. **Purchase Price**. The purchase price of the property was $70,000.00 with closing costs of $2,710.60 for a total of $72,710.60.

The parties obtained a loan on the property secured by a first deed of trust in the amount of $52,500.00. The balance of the purchase price and closing costs, the sum of $20,210.60, was supplied as follows:

```
FATHER   -   $18,750.00
SMITH    -   $ 1,460.60
```

2. **Carrying Costs**. The payments on the note secured by the first deed of trust shall be made by SMITH who shall also make payment on all taxes, insurance and other carrying costs of the property. The parties intend that since SMITH shall be responsible for said payments they shall be entitled to any tax deductions available by reason of said payments.

3. **Possession**. SMITH shall have the exclusive right to possession of the property so long as they are not in default under the terms of this Agreement or in default under any of the payments required to be made for principal, interest, taxes, insurance, or other carrying costs of the property. They shall not be required to pay rent.

4. **Failure to Make Payment**. In the event that SMITH fails to make their required contributions of principal, interest, taxes, insurance, or other expenses required by the property, FATHER shall have the right and option to make up such sums in default. In the event the party in default fails to cure the

default within thirty (30) days after the payment in default was due, then FATHER, having cured the default, shall have the option to purchase the interest in the property of SMITH for the price and terms set forth in the following paragraph.

5. **Death of a Party**. In the event that a party dies (in the event of SMITH, both JOHN and MARY), while all or any portion of the property remains unsold, the surviving party shall have an exclusive option for a period of sixty (60) days after the death of such party to purchase from their estate all of their title and interest in the property by giving a written notice of election to the personal representative of the estate of the deceased party or, if no personal representative be appointed, to a known heir of the deceased party. The purchase price shall be the decedent's share of the fair-market value of the property determined by (a) subtracting all encumbrances and liabilities against the property from the fair-market value; (b) crediting the decedent with their original capital contribution to the purchase price, any payments reducing the principal amount of the mortgage and the cost of any capital improvements; and (c) crediting the decedent with fifty percent (50%) of any appreciation in the value of the property or debiting the decedent with fifty percent (50%) of any depreciation in the value of the property. In the event the parties cannot agree as to the fair-market value, the same shall be determined by arbitration in accordance with the provisions of the California Arbitration Act, § 1280 *et seq.* of the California Code of Civil Procedure. If the surviving tenant in common elects to purchase said interest from the representative of the estate of the deceased party, they shall tender the option price to said representative within a period of ninety (90) days after notice of said determination of the option price. The representative of the estate of the deceased party shall petition for any court order and do all things necessary to complete said sale and conveyance. The deed or deeds shall be in the usual form of grant deed by the representative of the estate in proper statutory form for recordation, shall be duly executed and acknowledged so as to convey said interest in fee simple, free of all liens and encumbrances except those which are being assumed by the surviving party. If no election is made to determine the value of a deceased party's interest or said option is not exercised after said determination, then the representative of the estate of the deceased party may then sell said interest without further offers to the surviving tenant in common or other restrictions herein imposed, or distribute said interest to the persons entitled to under the Will of the deceased party or the applicable laws of intestate succession. In such event, the person acquiring the same shall assume the benefits and burdens of the deceased party under this Agreement and shall further be bound by all of the terms of this Agreement. The death of a spouse of one of the parties shall have no effect, it being the intent of the parties that in such event the surviving spouse shall assume all of the obligations and duties of the deceased spouse under this Agreement.

6. **Title**. As a matter of convenience, the parties have taken title to the real property in the names of SMITH alone. Notwithstanding said fact, it is understood and agreed that the SMITHS hold said property in trust as follows:

"JOHN SMITH and MARY SMITH, his wife, as to an undivided 50% interest as community property, and RICHARD FATHER, a married man, as to an undivided 50% interest as his sole and separate property."

On demand, SMITH shall execute and record a formal deed granting title as indicated above. Until such time, SMITH shall hold said property in trust pursuant to all of the terms and conditions of this Agreement.

7. **Sale or Disposition**. Except as otherwise provided herein, the unanimous agreement of all of the parties shall be required for the improvement, encumbrance, sale, or other disposition of the property. Except as provided herein, none of the parties hereto shall exchange, partition, lease, mortgage, convey by deed of trust, hypothecate, or otherwise encumber said real property or the interest owned by him therein, or any part thereof, or directly or indirectly, sell, transfer, or assign said property or his interest therein, or any part thereof, to any person other than a party hereto except with the written consent of all of the parties hereto first had and obtained, or upon the conditions herein set forth. Any such act prohibited shall be null and void and of no force or effect whatsoever.

8. **Relationship between the Parties**. The parties agree that the relationship between them with respect to said real property is and shall be that of tenants in common of an undivided interest, and that there is and shall be no partnership relationship between them and no party shall obligate or bind any other party with respect to said real property or in connection with any purchase, obligation, or indebtedness, except as provided herein.

9. **Successors**. This Agreement shall be binding upon the personal representative, heirs, beneficiaries, assigns, and successors in interest of the parties hereto, and the promises contained herein shall be considered covenants running with the land.

10. **Notices**. Any notice provided for herein shall be in writing and shall be given by depositing same in the United States mail, postage prepaid, addressed as indicated in the signature blocks hereto, unless the parties notify each other of a different address. Notice to the representative of the estate of a deceased party shall be addressed to him in care of his attorney of record in the matter of said estate.

11. **Attorneys' Fees**. In the event of any dispute arising hereunder, the prevailing party shall be entitled to reasonable attorneys' fees as may be fixed by a court of competent jurisdiction. Likewise, in the event of arbitration, the arbitrators may award attorneys' fees and otherwise apportion the costs of the arbitration proceeding; provided, however, that unless unusual circumstances prevail, the arbitrator shall award costs in proportion to the ownership of the undivided interest herein.

12. **Modifications**. All modifications of this Agreement shall become effective only when reduced to writing and signed by the parties.

13. **Termination**. Unless the real property subject to this Agreement is disposed of prior thereto, or the term hereof is extended by the mutual agreement of the parties in writing, this Agreement shall terminate five (5) years from the date hereof. At such time, SMITH shall purchase the interest of FATHER in accordance with the provisions of paragraph 5 set forth above or, if SMITH does not so elect, then FATHER shall have the option of purchasing SMITH's interest from them. If neither party elects to purchase from the other, said property shall be placed upon the market with a recognized multiple listing broker in accordance with the usual terms and conditions of Listing Agreements prevailing at that time. Any dispute as to sale price, terms, and like matters shall be resolved by binding arbitration under the provisions of the California Arbitration Act (C.C.P. §§ 1280 *et seq.*).

14. **Gain or Loss on Sale**. Any proceeds from the sale of said real property, whether occurring upon termination of this Agreement or by consent to mutual sale prior thereto, shall be distributed as follows:

(a) All encumbrances and costs of sale shall be paid.

(b) FATHER shall receive his initial contribution of $18,750.83, and SMITH shall receive their initial contribution of $1,460.60.

(c) SMITH shall receive all principal payments they have made on the purchase money encumbrance.

(d) SMITH shall receive the reasonable value or actual costs expended on any capital improvements made to the property as distinguished from ordinary maintenance costs. Any capital expenditures, to be recovered under this subsection, shall be approved by FATHER prior to the expenditure being made.

(e) The balance, if any, shall be shared as fifty percent (50%) to FATHER and fifty percent (50%) to SMITH. If the purchase price is not sufficient to pay both items (b) and (c), the proceeds shall be distributed pro rata to cover these items.

15. **Governing Law**. This Agreement and the rights and duties of the parties shall be governed by the laws of the State of California. California shall have personal jurisdictions of the parties; Marin County shall be the exclusive venue for any suit or action brought under this Agreement; and any suit or action shall be brought and thereafter prosecuted only in California State Courts.

IN WITNESS WHEREOF, the parties have hereunto set their hands on the dates indicated.

Date: _____   Date: _____

_____   _____
JOHN W. SMITH   RICHARD FATHER
1625 Happy Avenue   880 Las Gallinas Avenue
Sonoma, CA 95730   San Rafael, CA 94903

_____
MARY A. SMITH
1625 Happy Avenue
Sonoma, CA 95730

146

Disclaimer re inspectors:

The names of inspectors and other professionals listed above are given as a matter of accommodation only. The agents and brokers assume no responsibility for any act or omission on the part of the inspector or professional selected.

Boundaries:

The Broker has not been informed by Sellers of the precise boundaries of the property and neither Sellers nor Broker makes any representations regarding boundary locations or the size of the parcel except as may be shown on the preliminary title report. It is recommended that if purchaser has any questions in this regard, the purchaser should obtain a survey and also acquire an ALTA Owners' Title Insurance Policy which can give greater coverage than the CLTA Standard Coverage Policy. Your title company can explain the extended coverage and what additional cost, if any, is involved.

147

Rule Against Perpetuities:

Add the following phrase to all contingencies:

but not later than [date]

Abbreviated "As Is" Clause:

This property is being sold in an "AS IS" condition, with no representation or warranty made concerning its condition. Purchasers acknowledge that they have been cautioned to obtain inspections from qualified professionals as to the condition of the property, and have agreed to accept the property in an "as is" and "where is" condition. This provision supersedes all other provisions in this agreement regarding maintenance prior to close of escrow.

Maintenance:

The fact that a defect is disclosed in the property disclosure statement or by inspection shall not relieve the seller from the responsibility to correct said defect if otherwise provided in the purchase agreement.

148

Back-up Offer:

BACK-UP OFFER ADDENDUM

Buyer and Seller acknowledge that a primary agreement now exists on the subject property, and that this agreement is accepted in a secondary or back-up position under the following terms and conditions:

1. This contract shall become primary upon termination of the existing primary agreement. Termination does not occur until the primary offeror executes written cancellation instructions.

2. Until Buyer has received written notice the prior agreement has been terminated and this contract is in primary position:

   (a) Buyer may terminate this contract without liability by giving written notice to Seller or Seller's agent;

   (b) All time periods specified in this agreement will not begin to run;

   (c) Buyer need not open escrow or tender the down payment.

3. Seller reserves the right to extend or modify any and all terms and conditions of the primary agreement at Seller's discretion.

4. Unless placed in primary position with _____ days from the date hereof, this agreement shall terminate and be of no further force and effect.

Section 1031 Exchange:

Buyer agrees to accommodate seller in effecting a tax-deferred exchange under Internal Revenue Code §1031. Seller shall have the right, expressly reserved here, to elect this tax-deferred exchange at any time before closing date. Buyer agrees to execute all documents reasonably necessary in connection with such an exchange, provided that:

(a)   Buyer shall not be required to take title to any property, real or personal, other than the subject property;

(b)   such cooperation shall not delay the closing date;

(c)   such cooperation shall be at no cost or expense to Buyer; and

(d)   consummation of this agreement is not predicated or conditioned upon the exchange.

It is understood that neither the Buyer or the Brokers have given any advice to Seller concerning the exchange or the possible impact of any pending legislation.

Condominium Insurance:

Since Buyers own an interest in the common area as a tenant in common, they should obtain personal liability insurance in the event that the insurance carried by the homeowners' association is not adequate.

150

Table Of Authorities

CASES

151

152

153

STATUTES

155

TEXTS

Index

157

159

161

R

S

164

W

Z